Therapists
in the
Community

Therapists in the Community

Changing the Conditions that Produce Psychopathology

by

Matthew P. Dumont, M.D.

JASON ARONSON INC.
Northvale, New Jersey
London

THE MASTER WORK SERIES

1994 softcover edition

Copyright © 1968 by Science House, Inc.

Library of Congress Cataloging-in-Publication Data

Dumont, Matthew P.
    Therapists in the community : changing the conditions that produce
  psychopathology / by Matthew Dumont.
       p. cm.
    Includes bibliographical references.
    ISBN 1-56821-405-7
    1. Social psychiatry. 2. Community psychiatry. I. Title.
RC455.D78   1994
362.2'0425—dc20   94-37986

Manufactured in the United States of America. Jason Aronson Inc. offers books and cassettes. For information and catalog write to Jason Aronson Inc., 230 Livingston Street, Northvale, New Jersey 07647.

To the memory of C.G.D.

CONTENTS

The gods had condemned Sisyphus to ceaselessly rolling a rock to the top of a mountain, whence the stone would fall back of its own weight. They had thought with some reason that there is no more dreadful punishment than futile and hopeless labor.

The Myth of Sisyphus
Albert Camus

FOREWORD

It seems to me as though many years have passed since I was an intern in Brooklyn and was called to see a patient in a fifth floor slum tenement. After climbing the stairs with the ambulance attendant and two policemen who were there to protect me, I entered a room which appeared to be no more than 12 feet square. In it were about a dozen people joined by giant rats circling under the sink and cockroaches on the walls and ceilings. Under the single bulb which lit the room were people preparing food, children playing, couples performing sexual acts, people coughing, smoking—all huddled together in poverty and despair. In the far corner of the room was a woman lying in a pool of blood, having just delivered a baby and the after-birth. Spontaneously, without a thought, I turned to the ambulance driver—perhaps to cover my own anxiety —and asked, "Which one is the patient?"

Since that confrontation with poverty and the environment within which it existed, my path has taken a direction that to many seems unrelated, diverse, and perhaps irrelevant to the role of psychiatrist. My work as psychoanalyst, planner, and public health physician has involved me in concerns with city planning, government, cities, the poor, voluntary services, economics, and law. Cutting across all these microenvironments has obviously changed me as a psychiatrist from the classic psychiatrist model as perceived by other physicians and by the lay community. Many persons have questioned the relevance of my work to my professional training. To some, I seem to be whiling away my time at things totally apart from the concerns of a physician, and yet, man is part of his environment, irrevocably linked to all that is around. To others, as Matthew Dumont says of himself, I have become an "absurd healer."

Where once man was struggling to fight with the natural environment and all its dangers, man is now concerned, whether he is aware of it or not, with the environment which he himself has created. This environment has been put together by people, each operating independently and yet indirectly affected by others. All too often the environment has been created to meet needs far removed from man's actual needs.

Man is faced by ingrained needs, independent of his environment—needs for food and nurture, for love and for affection, for belonging and for the ability to master. Man needs to reproduce, to create; indeed the list of man's needs is lengthy. Many of these needs are so basic that society must provide for them in one form or another. Yet the very environment man has created to meet these needs —an environment made up of both physical things and social relationships—so modifies and changes him that his needs are either inadequately met or are warped. Furthermore, this environment creates new needs that force him to find new ways of coping. It has created smog and pollution so that man must now find ways to have water that is clean to drink and to play in. Thus, man's needs have multiplied and become more complex.

The psychiatrist who concerns himself only with his patient assumes he need not become concerned with the broad world. For many psychiatrists, the focus and concern must indeed be that of the individual patient. His concern with the broader environment is limited to how that environment impinges upon the patient and how the patient copes, adapts, and modifies himself to deal with it. The psychiatrist is concerned with increasing man's competence to deal with this environment and with increasing his patient's power to command the events that affect his life.

As Doctor Dumont points out, all too often the psychiatrist finds that no matter how much he attempts to deal with the individual, no skill now known permits him to make changes in the individual's behavior because the mix of individual and environment is such that individuality is overwhelmed by all that surrounds him. Only changes in the environment, both physical and social, can free the individual so that he can acquire the competence to move on and escape from powerlessness. Thus the therapist concerned with the individual may find himself concerned about other people, other programs, other activities that impinge upon his patient's life. Even in his preoccupation with the individual patient, he becomes a community psychiatrist.

The other extreme is the psychiatrist who is concerned not just with the patient, but with society at large. He is concerned with reducing the pathology in the total community. He is interested in optimizing the health and productivity and the creativity of the people. A psychiatrist with these concerns finds that what he is capable of doing in therapy is so infinitesimal an intervention that therapy alone cannot change the broader picture. He then enters into alliances, cooperatively and collaboratively, with people who have more impact on the environment, and thus on the individual, than he himself may have directly through therapy. It is at this point that the community psychiatrist enters the world that to many appears absurdly removed from his skills and his medical background. It is also at this point that the community psychiatrist becomes part of the politics of society.

The psychiatrist enters this new world as untrained, unskilled, frightened, and frustrated as I was when I entered the room in Bedford-Stuyvesant in 1949. To enter this new world the psychiatrist needs new skills and new working relationships. People like Doctor Dumont and myself have, in large part, learned the new skills of community psychiatry from experience plus a few opportunities for formal training and learning which are largely unavailable in the current training of the psychiatrist, the physician, or even the public health professional.

What Matthew Dumont records in this book is the response of a sensitive psychiatrist to the changes that are taking place in the world around him. The psychiatrists entering community psychiatry today are not unlike Freud and his followers in the Victorian period. They are aware that the existing institutions and modes of treatment and the way that society itself operates are no longer adequate to deal with the ever-changing problems of the society-at-large, and they are aware that mental illness and mental health are interrelated with these broad problems.

Doctor Dumont's book is not merely an indication that the field of psychiatry is in crisis and is forcing change upon its professionals, but also an indication, indeed, that every professional field—whether it be law or city planning, government or administration, finance or education, or a whole host of others that are concerned with our new urban existence—is in ferment. No single field can adequately deal with the problems as now defined because each is still dealing with problems defined by the past. Indeed, the profession of psychiatry is far from changing itself; it is being changed by events around it. Facts must be faced that are being brought to light by the stark reality of our confrontation with poverty and racism and the inadequacies of all our systems of care and concern for the human being.

Our attempts to solve these problems are far from adequate. We must redefine the problem and collect new data. We must make new connections; we must participate in processes that lead to change in ourselves and our institutions. We must create new institutions, new modes of behavior, and participate in the ever-evolving process of change.

The model of ecology is extremely useful in looking at Doctor Dumont's concerns. As a model of an open system that is ever-changing and completely interrelated, it helps man to avoid seeing the world as one with simple cause-and-effect responses in which simple solutions suffice. This model sees symptoms as tops of icebergs, and riots as only symptoms of vast underlying difficulties within the society-at-large. It sees our society not as one so sick that it must be destroyed by revolution or other means but as a society capable of revitalizing and retooling itself.

The ecological view recognizes that man has the inherent ability to modify himself through change. It helps the psychiatrist concerned with the processes of change in individuals to perceive and participate in the process of change in society. It enables him to recognize his limitations and his need for help from others and to recognize that the basic ability to make changes rests not in the therapist but in the people themselves who must find solutions to their own problems.

Doctor Dumont points to a new direction for all psychiatrists. His proclaiming himself an "absurd healer" is true only in that he seeks change of such purport as to make him appear absurd in comparison with the dimensions of that which is to be healed. He recognizes his antecedents. He has deep roots in psychiatry, and his work has come out of experiences with Erich Lindemann, Gerald Caplan, and others in the field. But more important than his psychiatric antecedents is his entrance into a host of other disciplines in which people are concerned with change.

While I was with the National Institute of Mental Health, I entered into a dialogue with many people concerned with man and his relationship to society with the purpose of expanding the concept of mental health from the narrow world of psychiatry to the much broader world of total politics. However, the concerns of NIMH which have led to its deep involvement with all behavioral sciences, with planning, economics, political science, architecture, and a host of other disciplines are but small drops in the professional pool. Matthew Dumont is picking up these concerns and is carrying them on in his involvement with social policy and planning, with gangs of Negroes, with kids working in urban slums, and with all his other activities upon which he has not even touched in this book.

Doctor Dumont does not consider his words here as the final words, nor does he expect them to be all inclusive. He is exposing himself, talking about his journey, his own experiences of moving into this new world. He is showing that there is a light which can lead the way along the path into the unknown. He is on a search for truth, though he knows within his heart that he will never find it and that this search will continue through his and all our lifetimes.

This search of his should serve as succour to all others who enter it unaided by precedent, as some of us did in the earlier days of community psychiatry. Doctor Dumont knows that although many professionals are linked to their profession by iron chains or to their bureaucracy by blind loyalty, there are others like him in many professions who are on the same search. It is in this colleagueship among the change agents, among the invisible colleges, in the floating crap game to which he refers, that he finds his support and his hope for the future.

This book is a very important one and one which should be read for more than the words alone; it should be read for the feelings and the emotions which lie between each of them, for each word brings images and associations that should start any aspiring community psychiatrist along this road toward a society which is concerned with human worth, dignity, and mental health.

Leonard J. Duhl, M.D.

PREFACE

At first this book was for me alone. It grew out of endless
dialogues within myself, insomniac reveries, memories of
forgotten hopes, a chaotic mixture of confusion and revelation. At great cost I had become a physician, after still
more of an effort, a psychiatrist, and now, as a community
psychiatrist, I have found myself drastically changing the
role model that had taken years of painstaking preparation.
My metamorphosis was like that of the child who gleefully
knocks down the tower of blocks he has constructed with
care and patience or perhaps like Sisyphus who with a
secret happiness watches his rock roll back down to the
depths. But as I began to write, the confusion became
more circumscribed, more finite. The redefinition of the

role model of physician and psychiatrist into community psychiatrist became less wantonly destructive. Writing helped me to see things in proper scale.

The recognition that some of my confrères in community psychiatry might want to share some of these thoughts spurred a more systematic attempt at writing. But the idea of a book, something so public, final and eternal, did not take shape before the recognition that the community psychiatrist-to-be would most value this kind of self-appraisal. It was then to medical students and psychiatric residents that I would direct this work.

The narcissism of an author is a terrible thing. Images of a frustrated and clamorous public appeared above the pages of the manuscript. What right did I have to ignore the intelligent lay readership hungry for new ideas and irreverent wisdom, especially if it had something to do with psychiatry. Psychoanalysis has been explaining itself to the general public for decades. Community psychiatry has as much of a right, perhaps even more of an obligation to put itself to public scrutiny. Of the specialties in medicine, community psychiatry above all is the province of laymen, it should have no option to develop an esoteric jargon because it speaks to the community rather than to its own brotherhood. It does not prescribe and command as does traditional medicine. It responds or persuades as does any other community agent. It does not reside within a temple but in the market place. It never stands alone—proud, solemn, august—but always seeks alliances—informal, comradely, egalitarian. With this in mind I again had to widen the target of readership. It was not only colleagues, present and future, who might want to witness these professional calisthenics, but also the general public.

As you can see, this had to be a very personal book. It is not scholarly, but there are some annotated references to guide the reader who wishes to be a bit more disciplined and systematic in his exploration of community psychiatry.

How does one begin or end acknowledging help for one's ideas? And how does one begin or end giving thanks to those who have sustained and supported the making of a book? I must at least mention the educators who have bequeathed me a legacy of wisdom and open-mindedness: Charles Frankel at Columbia; Knight Aldrich and his staff at the University of Chicago; Erich Lindemann, Gerald Caplan, and John Nemiah at Harvard. Leonard Duhl, of course, commands a special place as mentor and guide for me, for these ideas, and for all of community psychiatry. I shall always marvel with gratitude at the noble, wise, and inscrutable forces that brought together as my co-workers Harry Cain, Richard Wakefield, and Stephen Baratz. This association has made many things possible. Coryl Jones nurtured this manuscript with patience, devotion, and an incredible sense of what is or is not a communication. Despite Jason Aronson's judgment in deciding to publish a book such as this, our friendship has become even richer and deeper. And my wife has done nothing less than make all things worthwhile.

Matthew P. Dumont, M.D.

GENESIS OF A COMMUNITY PSYCHIATRIST

1

One spring day I leaned over a dying man and watched as his last breath was drawn through rotted teeth. I listened to a silent heart with a stethoscope, and then with the prerogatives and licenses granted by a state, a city, a hospital, a university, and a three thousand year old tradition, I pronounced that a human life had ended.

In the middle of a spring night several years later, I strained to hear the drugged and sobbing voice of a woman who had just tried to end her life. Her chronic and hopeless illness had suddenly taken a turn for the worse, leaving her helplessly and incontinently awaiting an imminent death. She preferred to die by a last assertion of will. The prerogatives and licenses of the physician remained, but they did not seem very important as one human being tried to tell another about life and death.

On a spring morning two years later, I walked from the bright sunlight into a gray and shadowy tavern where the air was heavy with the smell of beer and stale breath. I shook hands with the bartender, nodded to a decrepit man next to me, and drank beer as I listened to the conversation and observed the interaction among a half-dozen homeless men.

In the barroom I had neither license nor sanction. I had even less a year later when I spoke with the administrative assistant of a United States Senator about police harassment of a gang of Negro youths who had turned their attention from extortion to voter registration.

These episodes highlight a strange career development for a physician. It is a career that departs in ever-widening cycles from traditional medical practice. It is a move from the medical model of individual patient care to a position of responsibility for large populations and involvement with social forces.

As a psychiatrist I was to minister to the needs of suffering individuals in a role protected and supported by centuries of respect and ascribed authority. My behavior was to be ordered by a body of ethics that was almost sacred and directed by an unassailable tradition of medical science. And now . . .

Now I am a community psychiatrist and I function in an undefined role catering to undefined needs of an undefined clientele. This role has not been baptized by traditional medical prescriptions of confidentiality and responsibility. It is suspect among professional colleagues and responsive to no articulate demand from the community. I have moved from the respectable formality of psychodynamics to the ambiguity of politics and social change.

Where am I and how did I get here? Am I still a psychiatrist, still a physician? Or have I become an inadequately trained social scientist or some type of revolutionary?

I need to stand back for a moment, see what I am doing, and try to place what I find in a conceptual framework. I need to look at the forces that have propelled me in this direction. I need primarily to determine if the widening cycles of my departure from traditional medical practice are nonetheless securely rooted in that tradition. I need to do these things because it is inescapable that I will continue in the direction I am going.

The first challenge to my medical and psychoanalytically oriented focus on the individual patient was the residue of a social conscience. It was not a very large one, after all, but large enough to sensitize me to certain economic aspects of psychiatric care. It became very clear to me that psychiatry was a little inequitable. It is not just that 18,000 psychiatrists have preempted the job of looking after the millions of mentally ill, but that psychiatry's major treatment, psychotherapy, is predicated on social class. Psychotherapy, as generally practiced, requires a patient who is verbal, insightful and motivated, one who can delay gratification, and who, more or less, shares the values of the therapist, thereby virtually excluding the lower class person from treatment.

Psychiatrists are no more mercenary than other physicians, nor are they among the more affluent specialists. In other branches of medicine the *quality* of care will vary with the financial state of the patient, but only in psychiatry is the *method* of treatment determined by such factors.

A higher incidence of mental illness exists among the poor, and for this group there has been only the options of becoming psychotic and being hospitalized in a custodial institution or getting no care at all. Study after study has demonstrated the relationship between poverty and mental illness.[1] We cannot say with any more certainty that poverty causes mental illness than that cigarette smoking causes cancer. The correlations are there, but the intermediate variables of a causative relationship are absent, giving the apologists of tobacco, for example, sufficient grounds to maintain a controversy. If, however, the medical profession devotes all of its effort in combatting lung cancer to thoracic surgery and none of it to programs aimed at reducing cigarette smoking, it will lose the battle. In the same way, if it is determined that mental illness is caused by poverty or by unemployment or by social discrimination, then it will be the responsibility of the mental health professions to devote at least some of their attention to these issues or the battle against mental illness will be lost.

The proponents of individual psychotherapy as the only model of psychiatric intervention are on shakier ground than the surgeons. A surgeon may insist that public education and legislative action are not his areas of competence, but he does at least devote his knowledge and skills to the individuals most in need of his care. The psychiatrists who insist on the practice of psychotherapy, and on that alone as their *raison d'être,* generally devote their attention to a middle-class population, and for the most part only to the mildly neurotic within that population. A tremendous effort of education, a huge outlay of public and private funds, and a scarce supply of human intelligence and sensitivity is expended on a small number of persons who probably have the individual and social resources to function adequately without treatment. Concern for this group is more a matter of level of performance, but this is in the face of a picture of overwhelming individual, family, and social disintegration among the poor. It is fascinating that every index of mental illness is highest among the poor except psychoneurosis—the one condition most amenable to individual psychotherapy. Psychiatry has generated a middle-class treatment for middle-class patients.

With the rationalization that his techniques of psychotherapy should be utilized on only those persons for whom they do the most good, the psychiatrist condones an outrageous misallocation of human resources. The rationalization is a poor one. A specialty of medicine has the responsibility to elaborate new techniques if old ones cannot help the most needful population.

In the final analysis, asking for definite proof that poverty "causes" mental illness is asking for the impossible. Scientists among us are devoting their careers to finding "the cause" of mental disorders. How can there be a single cause of anything so complex as an arbitrarily defined collection of behavior characteristics? We are not so naive as to believe any longer that any historical act, a war or a revolution, for example, has a single cause. We can be philosophical and ask if any iota of fact, like the falling of an acorn, has a single, ultimate or final cause. Causation is a fiction, an absurd abstraction, superimposed on a panoply of events to give it the semblance of meaning, order, and direction.

We say that the tubercle bacillus causes tuberculosis and take comfort in what seems like hard, indisputable, rational fact. What is factual is that tuberculosis cannot exist without the bacillus, but two individuals exposed to the same number of bacteria can respond in different ways depending upon a whole variety of host and environmental factors, some known, some unknown. The response may be a fulminating disease leading to death or an asymptomatic immunity. Poverty is a "cause" of tuberculosis as much as is the bacillus.[2] Everything in medicine, everything in nature is the result of an infinite array of forces, actions, and reactions. Some of these are, however, more salient, immediate, potent, or remediable than others. Tuberculosis can be controlled by immunization or by early detection and treatment. It might also be controlled by the elimination of poverty.

To ask for definite proof that poverty causes mental illness is to deny that poverty acts as one of a number of salient influences on a set of behavior patterns which we call disordered. That poverty is highly correlated with these patterns has already been demonstrated. We know too little about the hereditary, biochemical, or developmental influences on these behavioral patterns to insist that the "truth" lies in these rather than in unemployment, segregation, anomie, inadequate housing or other aspects of social deprivation. Our responsibility as behavioral scientists is to determine which influences are more modifiable in their effects on specific patterns of behavior, not to determine which is the "true" cause.

The second train of thought that made it difficult

to sustain the individual patient model came from the investigations of psychiatrists themselves. There are many differences between physical illnesses and psychiatric disorders. A major one is that while organic disease is limited to the physical organism, to the skin and its contents, mental illness is just as much a phenomenon of the environment around the patient. The violently deranged patients that Philippe Pinel encountered in the Bicêtre Hospital in 1794 were less violent and less deranged when their chains were struck off. More recently it was found that a patient in a mental hospital had a psychotic deterioration because of a covert disagreement between her therapist and ward administrator.[3]

There is a village in Belgium called Geel where for a thousand years "possessed" patients have been cared for in the homes of peasants. My observations[4] of these patients demonstrated to me that the "social breakdown syndrome"[5] of chronic schizophrenics is more an expression of custodial hospitalization and social isolation than something inherent in the illness. The greatest part of the social disability of this illness may derive from the way schizophrenics are treated. In Geel, on the other hand, where the patients are almost entirely unrestrained and where the tolerance to deviant behavior in the community is extraordinarily high, schizophrenia does not appear to be a very disabling illness. Apparently the degree of psychosis is related to the social and interpersonal setting of the patient.

The implications of these observations are more staggering than the statement of them. These observations mean, in short, that *mental illness does not entirely reside within the individual.* Community psychiatry, if nothing else, is an attempt to determine just how much of mental illness resides outside the individual, but this hurries my story too much. Conceptual leaps take place in small steps and it is only in retrospect that they are recognized at all.

Another major development from psychiatric research and practice added to the momentum of change: studies of family dynamics and attempts to treat the entire family as a unit. At first this was felt to be a new and effective way of approaching emotionally disturbed children. Soon, however, observers began to perceive a whole new dimension of psychopathology, i.e., disturbed relationships. The double-bind[6] was described as a situation in which contradictory messages are sent by a parent to a child in such a way that the contradiction cannot be recognized. It is as if a mother were to slap her child's hand as he reached for a piece of candy, and as the child withdraws his hand, his mother were to mutter, "You weakling."

In family dynamics it was too tempting to see explorations of such disturbances as attempts to find the "really sick one" in the family as other than the identified patient. A recently published and highly popularized book[7] which analyzes stereotyped relationships between people as "games" falls into this trap of looking for the real villain. Other therapists have gone further than this, and rather than see one or the other family member as the carrier of pathology or the focus of treatment, they have seen the patterns of communication, the interaction itself, as the disturbance. The "illness" was not within family members but between them.

One of the first families I had in treatment revealed this to me. A 17-year-old boy was sent to the clinic with a family friend who was to communicate to the psychiatrist the concerns of the boy's parents who themselves "could not make" the appointment. Their complaints, as communicated second-hand, were about the abrupt onset of the patient's argumentativeness, refusal to perform household obligations, and withdrawal from family life except for his incessant and belligerent demands to take over the family car and television set. The boy presented with a peculiar smile something between bravado and a smug, secret knowledge. He had strange repetitive gestures as if he were constantly picking minute, objectionable particles from his clothing. He said little other than giving evasive, disjointed answers to questions. Occasionally his sentences would become incomprehensible or suddenly stop midway. He acted indifferent to his parents and their complaints about him. A clinical impression of incipient schizophrenia was made but this diagnosis became less relevant when the family was prevailed upon to undertake treatment along with the patient.

This picture developed. For many years the mother had suffered from a chronic illness that required many operations, most of which left her more disabled and finally in endless pain. Despite her suffering, she never complained. She had a stiff-upper-lip attitude, never giving in to feelings of despair or hostility. She retained a childlike faith in her physicians despite their inability to relieve her. She was an "ideal" patient, even if she did not get better. Father was pillar of respectability, morality, and restraint. He stood by his wife with utter devotion and patience. He never permitted himself the slightest feeling of resentment towards his wife nor the barest wish to break away and find himself a mate who might be able to share the sexual, homemaking, and companionship aspects of marriage. They had two children, a year apart. The younger child, a girl, had nearly died in early childhood from rheumatic fever. Both parents spent sleepless nights for many months nursing her through her critical illness. They subsequently overprotected and catered to her and became terrified whenever she caught a cold. In the midst of this atmosphere of suffering, protectiveness, and selflessness, the son attempted to forge an identity for himself. Every normal impulse towards self-indulgence and every inclination to jealousy or hostility was laden with so much guilt by his parents' attitudes that he began to believe that he was evil. He found that he could not control his wishes and instincts so well as everyone else around him, and so he sought a sense of mastery by monopolizing the family car which he drove with endless fascination. He did well at school and spent many hours helping teachers or engaging in scout or religious activities. His symptoms began on the day that his sister got her driving license and demanded her share of the family car. As he fought for his need to preempt the only thing in the family he could master, he was made to feel more and more selfish. A vicious cycle developed as he acted increasingly like the image that was imposed upon him. The epitome of his role was described by Father as the day when Mother had to be hospitalized for an infection at the site of an operation. Father approached the boy and, as if to get him to repent his sins and act like the concerned, helpful, generous child they had hoped to procreate, asked him if he wanted to see his mother's infection. The boy "arrogantly and callously" refused. According to Father, and with the tearful acquiescence of Mother and the self-righteous in-

dignation of the daughter, the boy "didn't give a damn."
It seemed as if the boy were the bearer of every vile, base,
deprived, angry, and self-indulgent instinct in the family
while the rest could carry on in their pure, guiltless suffering. Where was the focus of pathology? Who was the sick
one? In whom was the illness when the illness lay in a
family myth that anger and resentment are evil, when it
lay in an unspoken, unrecognized conspiracy to expel hostility even if it meant expelling one of them with it? It
was to this that the treatment was directed.

Measured dosages of confrontation with their own
anger were administered to the parents. Anger was taught
to be legitimate and benign, first when directed at the
therapist and then at each other. They recognized with
difficulty that one can be angry at someone for being sick,
as unreasonable as this seemed, and it was seen not to be
catastrophic. They had a reshuffling of "goodness and bad-
ness" and looked at themselves and each other in less stereotyped and rigid ways. When the parents could comfortably recognize hostility in themselves, they saw less in their
son. Now they could understand that his disinclination
to see his mother's infection was not because he did not
care, but because he cared too much. The boy's symptoms
abated and the diagnosis changed from "schizophrenic
reaction" to "situational reaction of adolescence."

Still another professional encounter challenged the
old psychiatric model. I spent one year as psychiatric consultant on a physical rehabilitation ward. Here were not
psychiatric patients, not the mentally ill, just people. They
were generally young men and women who would spend
many months getting physical and occupational therapy:

quadruplegics, hemiplegics, amputees, or multiple sclerotics. They were paralyzed, limbless, or in constant pain. They would never again be normal.

As I listened to them talk and watched them struggle, I found it increasingly difficult to formulate what I saw along psychopathological, or even psychodynamic lines. It was not that these were irrelevant, but they seemed so much less important than the existential reality of human beings trying to cope with an overwhelming stress.

Psychiatrists have a sense of understanding and mastery about the fantasy life of their patients. We can interpret dreams and explain the influences of unconscious wishes and fears on human behavior. But to the psychiatrist, the forces of reality are dark and inscrutable. What a paradox! To others it is the world of dreams and hidden thoughts and discordant behavior that are strange and frightening, but to psychiatrists, it is the reverse!

Psychiatrists tend to focus on the past. The more psychoanalytically oriented the doctor is, the more distant the past upon which he focuses. With these rehabilitation patients, the past continued to exert its influence, but that influence was unpredictable and much less salient than I had been led to believe. The here and now and the future seemed so much more important. They were faced with a greater stress on their coping resources than they had ever faced before, a crisis of incredible intensity. Psychoanalytic theory could not adequately explain why some patients were able adequately to grieve their losses and carry on despite them, to seek what fulfillment life had yet to offer them, while others became chronically depressed or denied unrealistically that a loss had ever taken place. To some patients this confrontation with a terribly harsh reality provided them with the means for a personality development that they had never had before. This served to confirm the ancient wisdom of the Chinese whose word for crisis is made up of two characters, one depicting danger and the other opportunity.

I learned some bad psychiatric habits from this experience—or at least some of my colleagues thought they were bad. When I returned to the psychiatric clinic, I found myself drawing more attention to the day-to-day reality of my patients' lives than to the intricacies of their early psychosexual development. I continued to believe that psychoanalytic formulations illuminated much of what I heard and saw, but I began to feel that the loneliness of a retired old man, the emptiness in the life of an unoccupied suburban housewife, and the realistic dread in a Negro welfare recipient that her child's face would be bitten by a rat, were better explanations of depression and anxiety than unresolved pregenital conflicts.

These, then, were the three forces that unsuited me to the psychoanalytic model of a mental health career: a social conscience, the interpersonal and sociological revelations in psychiatry itself, and finally a conviction that ongoing reality was a more salient influence on human behavior than fantasies rooted in the past.

But an emptiness remained in my second vision of psychiatry.

THE SOUND OF ONE HAND CLAPPING

2

Something is lost and something is gained with every change. Among the things that were lost for me in my turning from the old medical model of psychiatry was a well circumscribed and neat conceptual framework for practice.[1] It was, of course, its very neatness and circumscription that drove me from it. But it was so convenient to be able to explain all observed behavior on the basis of psychoanalytic tenets. One can "explain" the most peculiar and complex interactions and verbalizations with a fair knowledge of psychoanalytic theory, a thorough knowledge of its jargon and a bit of sangfroid. Every psychiatric resident in an analytically oriented training program learns sooner or later with more or less awareness what a whore a psychodynamic formulation is. Anyone can use it for just about anything.

I must be very plain, despite my rhetoric, about a balanced view of psychoanalysis: it is a brilliant light in a darkened room, but the dark room of human problems is vaster than can be illuminated by that light. Poverty is not a masochistic triumph, and a psychoanalyst who implies that it is becomes a bedfellow of the 19th Century capitalist who felt that the reason his downtrodden workers were not where he was had to do with a deficiency of thrift and fortitude within them.

I do not want to belabor the point that human problems are not predominantly of intrapsychic origin. What I must look at with care and patience is whether or not, as a psychiatrist, I should have anything to do with those human problems which originate from outside the individual.

You know my answer. Let me seek reasons for it.

There was a basic assumption in the old model that the ego exists, that there was some independent variable known as the self. This seems to be a basic assumption of all human thought. In fact, it is not. The existence and preeminent importance of the self—the individual psyche—is a concept with which we have grown so much at home that it has become more than sacrosanct. It has become assumed to be universally true, but it is a peculiarly Western and particularly modern concept. A little thought will suggest how parochial an idea it is.

Individuals, we say, are embedded within various spheres of influence, such as the family, the community, the working environment, the church. We may grant that these spheres of influences have some kind of impact on the individual, but we maintain that there is a hard core of identity, of self-hood, that exists in that person under any circumstances. Diagrammed, it looks like this:

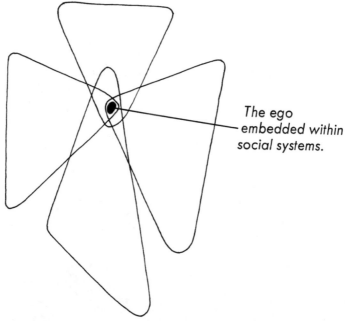

The ego embedded within social systems.

The individual exists within a number of fields of interaction. He may feel a richness or poverty of experience depending on the variety and intensity of these fields of interaction, but his continued existence remains a given reality.

Why is this inherently true or more meaningful than the Zen Buddhist concept of the nonexistence of the self?[2] This concept is simply an alternative and a no less meaningful way of describing the human condition. In this model, the individual is no more nor less than the confluence of fields of interaction. In diagram, it looks like this:

38

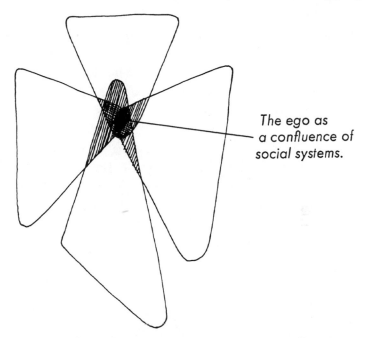

The ego as
a confluence of
social systems.

In this situation, when you remove one field of interaction, you remove part of the self; and as you strip more and more away, you are left not with a hard core of personal identity, but with nothing.

When the Zen master says the "self is like the sound of one hand clapping," he means that it is as impossible to conceive of the self without the environment as it is to conceive of the sound of one hand clapping without the other hand. In other words, while from a physical point of view, the skin may be said to distinguish between the self and the non-self, from a psycho-social point of view, the distinction is arbitrary and often artificial.[3]

We must be aware of how much violence this does to our accustomed ways of thinking about people. We still hang on to a kind of homunculus conception of identity in which a tiny primordial human being resides within the fertilized ovum, that within the genetic map of the human egg there lies an itinerary of human behavior. Of course, this is absurd. All that has been predestined is an array of biological equipment and an unknown potential for behavior. Obviously, much of that potential is biological in that a certain admixture of amino acids may result in mental retardation or schizophrenia or genius. But behavior remains to be determined by its existence within the lifetime of the human result of the fertilized egg. Most mental retardation is from "cultural deprivation," not biological defect; schizophrenia cannot be adequately explained on genetic grounds; and genius may be dormant or destructive depending on its use or lack of use.

The essence of human behavior does not precede its existence. This is an existentialist restatement of the humanistic faith in freedom from predetermination. The possibilities of our existence are greater than its actuality.[4]

All of these and many more fancy thoughts emerge when one does not have a fixed view of an individual's nature. Change a man's environment and you change the man. Provide the opportunity for a rich life and the individual becomes rich; conversely, restrict opportunity and you have a constricted individual. From a purely intellectual point of view, it is hard to deny the weight of evidence to this interpersonal or transactional perspective. The study of human behavior strongly suggests that we are little more than a concatenation of interactions and that psychosocially speaking the line between the self and the environment is entirely arbitrary. It is so tempting, however, to say that both perspectives are true in their own way. This is a safe philosophy, and the most exciting thing you can say about it is that it is probably right.

On the other hand, our emotional and intuitive conviction of the primacy of individual identity is a bit of data we cannot ignore. With the immediacy and urgency of a conversion experience, everything within us invokes a belief in the reality and a sacred commitment to the importance of individual life. Perhaps to the social scientist, grief and love are roles and behavioral sets, and to the Zen Buddhist, fields of interaction. But the lover knows whom he loves and the bereaved knows for whom he grieves. Those of us not in love and not grief-stricken may knowingly stand aside and comment to ourselves how these feelings come and go. We may note ironically how quickly passion becomes ennui as if, in fact, it were the role of the beloved or the mistress or the other man's wife that was loved—rather than a person. But when we are in love or grieving, do not mention roles—tell us only about the one for whom we yearn.

Perhaps this is why there is room for the physician in endeavors of social study and social change. He brings to the arena of interpersonal and transactional thinking a firm commitment to the importance of the individual and an irrevocable sensitivity to his suffering.

There is something a little unconscionable about the social scientist. In his very attempt to be objective and free of prejudice, in his need to be free of values, there results a sterile accuracy, a dehumanized precision that makes his conclusions a shade less than valid. The case history is in disrepute among social scientists. They prefer extensive surveys in which standards of reliability can be maintained. They seem to feel that many cursory answers to a question provide more truth than a focus on one person's subtle and conflicted reactions to the question. But the case history, the classical approach of the medical model, does not provide less, but truth of a different kind. It is a little like the traditional military attitude toward casualties: one death is a tragedy; ten thousand deaths are a sanitation problem. Bare statistics persuade us of nothing. What does it mean that several hundred thousand people will starve in India? But show us a picture of one emaciated child looking into the anguished face of his mother!

Feeling tones of behavior is what the case study can provide. The unquantifiable qualities of human life, those that help make it distinctly human, are lost to the surveys of social scientists; these can be provided by adherents to the medical model.

If there is a place for the medical model in social science, then what of its role in social change? This need hardly be said. The history of mankind is full of revolutions beginning in an atmosphere of idealistic love of man and ending in a heartless destruction of men. A period of social change, whether revolutionary or evolutionary, requires a constant monitoring of its effect on individuals. There is no room for discussions of means and ends in the medical model. Human beings are never means to ends. The presence of a proponent of the medical model in discussions of social change is a constant reminder of the superordinate goal of all planning: the well-being of individuals, all of them, each of them. It is no accident that the hero of *Dr. Zhivago* is a physician as well as a poet.

Revolutionary fervor results in an adversarial, good-

guys-bad-guys orientation. The physician whose obligation is to treat all men acts as a modifying force. Perhaps
in a world that alternately celebrates and condemns revolutions, there is no place for a modifying force. Perhaps
the medical model is quietist and essentially antirevolu-
tionary because it sees pain, frustration, and death independent of the institutional arrangements about which
revolutions make so much noise. Perhaps there is a sense
of irrevocable sadness at the prospect of violent change,
with the knowledge that all men are brothers in suffering
and that the victim shares with the criminal a common
burden of human guilt. Perhaps this is a lot of nonsense,
but how far are these thoughts from the uncomfortable
knowledge every physician has that a murderer or a bigot
or a tormenter of men has as much demand of his loving
care as a man of virtue and nobility?

The community psychiatrist has not abrogated the
medical model. It is precisely because he harbors so much
of that model that his role is crucial among social planners.
A highly defensible urban renewal program may uproot
thousands of families for a socially desirable end; it remains for the community psychiatrist to look through the
plans for the city beautiful and ask about the health and
happiness of the uprooted. He straddles social science,
public health, and medicine. The first provides the range,
the second the methodology and the third . . . the conscience.

But health and happiness are not psychiatric terms.

WHAT IS MENTAL HEALTH?

3

What is mental health? The question becomes more and more obtrusive and our inability to answer it, more and more embarrassing.

Why do we have so much trouble with the question? Why can't we adopt some practical and operational maxims that will put an end to the annoyance? Is it because the role society has given us as physicians to the mentally ill does not come with the sanction to speak of the healthy? Have psychiatrists been stigmatized, stereotyped, and banished along with their patients, or has our banishment been self-imposed? Have we accepted this exile as the only possible rapprochement with society because if we

were to turn our attention to society itself we might see
. . . what madness?

Those of us who have gone beyond psychopathology,
who see only a spectrum between "normal" and "disturbed" behavior rather than a sharp line, may speak of
adaptation. We feel comfortable with this term. Some
people adapt better than others. The schizophrenic has
adapted less well than the neurotic who has adapted less
well than . . . the normal person, and with the maladapta-
tion there is distress. This is very neat and only slightly
untrue. But it isn't its lack of truth that sticks in our
throats, it is what is still left unsaid about that normal,
well-adapted, undistressed person.

What is adaptation to an absurd reality? What is
tranquility in an outrageous reality? We have been en-
dowed with the peculiar ability to observe and comment
critically on our own behavior. This critical faculty causes
us alternately, at times simultaneously, to love and hate
ourselves. It is only in the abrogation of the critical faculty
that we can be perfectly well adapted and in no pain.
Awareness itself brings distress, for it is of conflict and
frustration that we become aware.

The lobotomized patient feels no distress, and with
the refinements in neurosurgery he may be very well
adapted to his environment. He has been cleansed of the
bad depressive feelings. He may also have been cleansed
of the potential to weep at a sad movie or to grieve for
a lost friend.

The ability to feel sadness is the ability to feel compassion and probably the ability to feel love. Euphoria is
not a normal state for mankind, and it is one of the

troubling discoveries of psychiatry that the state of ecstasy is most common among schizophrenics.

Is it possible that adaptation itself may at times be pathological? There are facets of contemporary life in which our critical faculty instinctively rebels against a too facile adaptation. There have been environments in our recent history to which we should not have adapted so well as we did. Adaptation is a kind of acquiescence. Peace of mind demands freedom from conflict, and freedom from conflict is the abject slavery of unconscionable conformity.

I remember seeing a film a few years ago called *Mafioso,* directed by Alberto Latuada, that carried a subtle and unsettling message. The film opens in a huge, modern factory in Milan in which unnamed products are produced at great speed and efficiency. Alberto Sordi appears in a white coat carrying a stop watch around his neck. He is a time-motion expert adjusting the activity of the human elements of the industrial complex to the demands of the machines. He quickens the pace of a worker here, slows it there so that every movement is precise, coordinated, unwasteful, and responsive only to the needs of the whole, like one huge, staggeringly efficient machine combining organic and mechanical elements in a single, harmonious system.

The story takes its hero back, on vacation, to the Sicilian village where he was born. He is with his beautiful Scandinavian wife and two young children. We learn that as a boy he was a favorite of the local "don," a Mafia chieftain to whom faded aristocrats and peasants alike owed an absolute fealty. The hero's obligations to the don are intense because his job in Milan was evidently ar-

ranged for him. Sordi's wife sees the evidences of absolute
control and intolerance to defiance by the Mafia, but he
prefers to ignore or rationalize them, and, as the film is
ostensibly a comedy with a light tone, the viewer too can
accept them comfortably, i.e., without a sense of outrage.

As the story unfolds, Sordi is selected by the don for
an unknown task to be accomplished during one night.
Within a few short hours we see him thrust from one
mysterious rendezvous to another until he is placed in a
crate and flown to New York. There he attends meetings
whose purpose he cannot fathom and therefore with which
he cannot sympathize. The end of this synchronized
planning and activity is his standing at the doorway of a
barber shop in New Jersey, firing a gun at a man he has
never before heard of nor seen.

The hero is whisked back to Sicily with the same
efficiency and returns to his still sleeping wife with sobs
choking in his throat. He has become a murderer. The
film ends back in the factory, white coat and stop watch
as before, the rhythmic throbbing of the industrial machine blending with the distant strains of a Sicilian melody.

Every impulse of the viewer is not to see the hero
as a murderer. He has charm and warmth and appears
to have no instinct for evil. At the moment that he recognizes that his mysterious task is to kill a man who has
offended the Mafia "operta," his impulse is to fight and
escape; but as in every organization, sanctions can be applied and the subtle threat of harm to his family is enough
of a spur to the already established momentum that an
act of murder is the outcome.

The message of the film is not that a man will kill
rather than permit his family to be harmed. That would

47

involve a conflict of human instincts, a moral dilemma that each man must solve (or hopefully avoid having to solve) within his own soul. The more terrible message in this story is that human instincts themselves can be systematically eclipsed or made irrelevant within the framework of organizational goals.

Max Weber would have seen the essential *gesellschaft* similarity between the Milanese factory and the Mafia. The men in each system are not ends in themselves.

Mafia killings seem far away from polite society and a movie is, after all, just a movie, but there have been historical events in this vein which have left indelible marks on the history of mankind. That the culture of Goethe and Mozart could also produce the Third Reich's final solution testifies to the unaccountable wanderings of civilization.

It remained for Hannah Arendt[1] to put the phenomenon in its proper and most terrible perspective. Eichmann need not have been a monster to be a significant part of a monstrous phenomenon. He may well have been a man of ordinary conscience and sensitivity, *all too ordinary*, obeying orders, working diligently and efficiently to do what was expected of him to satisfy organizational goals. It was his very lack of individuality within the context of a smooth, taut, and efficient bureaucratic system that is horrible.

Eichmann's behavior is more horrible than that of a psychotic murderer because it is so familiar. His face showed the lines of routine, not of rage. The face merges with that of the Milanese efficiency expert, and either or both faces merge so easily with our own.

Mental health cannot be defined until a basic question

is answered. Is it to be defined in accordance with standards of normal behavior that society itself determines, or is its definition to be a challenge to those standards? Are mental health professionals the agents of previously defined normative standards or critics of them? Certainly our job would be easier if we assumed the former position. Society has decided that war is sensible and just but that rioting is not. Society condones certain ways of modifying our consciousness and condemns others. Society permits the public to be entertained by murder but not by lovemaking. The contradictions of communal life need not concern us if we merely accept as our own the prejudices of every thoughtless tradition in our culture. But perhaps there is an abrogation of responsibilities in our blind acceptance of arbitrary standards of normalcy.

Psychiatrists are a part of society in a more significant way than as instruments of it. We should have as much to say about its standards as any other part, and perhaps our contributions may be more meaningful than others because of our knowledge about conflict, motivation, and group process. To say that a psychiatrist has no greater right to comment upon our foreign or domestic policy than any other citizen is accurate, but that is also to say that he has as much right. There have been some who felt that psychiatrists should deny themselves even that right because they may be listened to with an ascribed authority greater than they deserve. I do not agree. While we may constantly remind society of the limitations of our disciplines, we cannot afford the luxury of sitting in a value-free grandstand.

What, then, is mental health? From what I have just

said, it can be expected that my definition will be arbitrary, subjective, and value-laden. It is also extraordinarily unoriginal.[2] Mental health is freedom.

Mental health is the widest conceivable range of choice in the face of internal and external constraints. The freedom of the neurotic is restricted by the internal constraints of repetition-compulsions, stereotyped perceptions, expectations of doom, or inordinate despair. The freedom of the psychotic is limited by his inability to distinguish between stimuli from within and those from without. In the same way, the freedom of the slum dweller is limited by poverty, unemployment, and segregation. In all cases, the final common path is a restriction of opportunity and a narrowness of choice. The purposes of psychotherapy and social change are to widen the range of possibilities, to increase the options of human behavior. In short, to enhance freedom.

I do not mean the personal freedom to do whatever one likes. If man's identity is to a large degree determined by his environment, then his highest aspirations are similarly determined. The slaveowner is no more free than his slaves because the range of his behavior is limited by his role as the owner of men. The slaveowner and his slave are in the same field of interaction and that field restricts both of them from interacting in different ways.

A man can rape a woman but he cannot force her to love him. He can, in fact, forever lose the possibility of her love by the act of rape. Whose freedom has been restricted? If freedom exists in the realm of the potential rather than the actual, then the restriction is never in one direction.

In this sense, freedom is not a matter of will. For the

50

purposes of action, we must recognize that the Nazis imposed their will on six million Jews. From the perspective of a theory of mental health, the Germans did violence to themselves as well as to the Jews. The Third Reich enslaved itself along with the Jews, and perhaps with all mankind at the same time.

There is no limit to the size of our fields of interaction. A very large and amorphous community can be a very viable one. At times our commonality as human beings is our most important source of identity. This is what I meant when I said that the victim shares a common burden of guilt with the criminal. When faced with some of mankind's crimes, his mass murders and wholesale exploitations, his holy wars and plunder, what other reaction can we have than to raise our hands to our heads and ask, "What are we doing to ourselves?" When we remember with a shock of recognition that all men are brothers, we cannot help but feel within our own souls the murmurings of every criminal instinct in history.

The freedom I write about is not unrestricted individual initiative but the shared aspiration for the widest range of possibilities for all men. I call this aspiration mental health.

THE CITY AS PATIENT

4

Having chosen a professional course that departs from the medical model but constantly invokes it and having chosen a goal so universal in its meaning as to be almost meaningless, what remains for me to do is fix this amorphous mass of thought to a more concrete target. For this I have chosen the city.

The problems of metropolitan existence have become increasingly urgent; it has become a cliché that they have reached crisis proportions. The urban situation is, then, a salient concern for this new discipline, and beyond this, it is a conceptually attractive one. The city can be seen as an ecological unit, as an organism capable of health or suffering.

It isn't too difficult to view the city in this way. Like any organism it has a circulatory system in its streets, railroads, and rivers; a brain in its universities and planning offices; a digestive system in its food distribution and sewerage lines; muscles in its industrial centers; and any city worthy of the name has an erogenous zone.

The major problem in the analogy is, that while in the human organism the total is clearly more important than any of its parts, in the city the single cells are human beings whose importance is preeminent.

The first question a physician must ask himself about an organism is whether it is suffering or not. There would seem little doubt that the urban organism is indeed distressed; it is feeling symptoms. There have been choking sensations, blackout spells, uncontrolled and uncoordinated growth patterns, and painful tissue destruction. By the last, of course, I mean the riots that have become the most conspicuous part of summertime in the city.

A riot is, however, a symptom of pathology and not pathology itself. Every physician is taught about the hazards of treating a symptom rather than the disease behind it. Pain may be deadened with a narcotic while undetected cancer continues to grow; a fever may be lowered while an infection continues to smoulder; and a depression may be lifted while an unresolved grief reaction continues to manifest itself in other ways. A purely symptomatic approach to distress can mean the death of the organism.

Symptoms are interesting phenomena. They not only indicate pathology but also frequently represent attempts on the part of the organism to self-correct the disturbance. Fainting, for example, is a symptom of a sudden lowering of blood flow to the brain. When the individual falls, the blood flow does not have to work against gravity, the pressure is stabilized, and the fainting spell is over. Inflammation is a symptom of infection, but with the increased temperature and expansion of the vascular supply that go along with inflammation, there is a more effective destruction of the invading bacteria. Coughing is not only a symptom or indicator of an obstruction to pulmonary air flow but also the most effective means of clearing it. On the other hand, under certain circumstances, symptoms may cause problems themselves. A fainting spell on a roof can cause death. A fever, if too high, may destroy brain tissue and cause death. An inflammatory reaction can destroy an eye or interfere with breathing.

What can we do with this analogy? Let us assume that a riot is a symptom. Can any new information or implications be derived? Is there any heuristic payoff to this game?

I see the inner-city riot as the indicator and partial corrector of four basic deficits in the urban organism.

There is a basic human need for *stimulation*. The phenomenon of sensory deprivation psychosis is well established. If you put a normal person into an atmosphere where there is little or no sensory stimulation, he will, in about 12 hours, hallucinate, become paranoid, think in a chaotic and disorganized way, in short, be as psychotic as a schizophrenic. Of course, it is reversible, but it is remarkably consistent, and no one is immune from it.

There have been clinical situations that mirror this experimental one. One of the best known phenomena in ophthalmology used to be known as the "black patch psychosis." When older persons were subjected to cataract surgery and would have to spend several days with eye patches, it was common for them to become suddenly quite disturbed. They would become suspicious, or scream out for no reason, or try to tear their bandages off, or become disoriented to time or place. It was discovered that turning on a radio or frequent verbal interchanges with a nurse sufficed to prevent this psychosis. It was nothing more than a sensory deprivation psychosis.

There is an interesting condition known among the Eskimos called "kayak *angst.*" It is known to every tribe that if a seal hunter had to spend many hours sitting in a kayak poised to spear his prey, he would suddenly act in a highly disturbed and dangerous way—screaming hysterically or actually jumping into the water. The situation of the hunter who silently waits in a small boat in an unruffled Arctic sea, nothing on the horizon but a thin rim of ice, the grayness of the sky merging with that of the water is, of course, made to order for a sensory deprivation psychosis and that is exactly what happens. Eskimo tradition calls for an intermittent singing or a vigorous rowing to prevent this illness.

There is in all of us a biopsychological hunger for stimulation as basic and urgent as our need for food and water.

. . . And what of the ghetto? Superficially, to the outsider, it would seem to be anything but a monotonous environment. There is an appearance of activity in the streets—children playing, men standing around on the street corners talking, an atmosphere of restlessness, excitement, and vitality. Saturday night in the ghetto, for example, is notoriously a time of release, of permitted excess. There is an aura of anticipation, as if passion or violence were around every corner. This would seem to be the farthest thing from stimulus hunger.

In fact, this atmosphere of intense vitality and violent passion is created out of the anxiety and hysteria of the outsider. The residents of the ghetto themselves describe a life of monotonous and unremitting changelessness. Hour after hour, day after day, unemployed men stand on street corners waiting for something to happen.[1]

The physical environment may seem novel and interesting to the white, middle-class suburbanite, unaccustomed to tenements and abandoned cars and garbage in the streets, but living among unchanging misery is as dull as living among unchanging comfort. South Central Los Angeles is an extreme example, but what is particularly upsetting about that ghetto is that while going through block after block after block of unattached bungalows, each with its yard or two of grass, unbroken by any interruption in the horizon, or focuses of commerce or changes in density, one begins to feel the nightmarish sense of having entered the block one has just left. It takes two and one-half hours to get to downtown Los Angeles from Watts by public transportation and there is not even a movie theater in the area. The psychological map, the itinerary of behavior of the ghetto resident is much more restricted than that of the white middle class.

The most salient aspect of the stimulus deprivation in the ghetto community, the feature that gives ghetto life its quality of chronic depression, is the lack of expectation of change. There is a sense of futurelessness that makes activity indifferent, pointless, perfunctory, and invariable.

Yes, Saturday night comes as a relief, and energies seem mobilized for a while. But Saturday night comes with terrible regularity and so quickly becomes Sunday morning.

Whatever else a riot is or does, at least something is happening. One source of the exhilaration among rioters, the "carnival atmosphere" that offends so many people, is that an input of stimulation is being provided where there is a desperate need for one. I would suggest that if we want to take riots away from the life of the inner-city Negro, we had better have a pretty good substitute in a source of activity or excitement.

A second basic psycho-social need, the frustration of which is behind the symptomatology of rioting, is *self-esteem*. Psychiatrists know that an acute loss of self-esteem can be catastrophic and is a frequent cause of suicide. We have also seen the debilitating effects of a chronically diminished sense of self-esteem in our patients.

We need to think well of ourselves. We need to be loved or respected or feared. We force ourselves to compensate for deficiencies imposed upon us. We paint or primp or exercise ourselves, we modulate our voices and modify our ideas and even distort our perceptions to fit our idealized self-image. We go through many performances that have apparent purposes other than the true one, which is to reassure ourselves that we are worthy of the love of others and of ourselves. In the final analysis we lie to ourselves, for when all fails and we are confronted with our naked reality, the pain can be overwhelming.

Little has to be said about the legacy of shame, the overdetermined deficiency of self-esteem of the inner-city

Negro. Physical bondage followed by economic bondage followed by welfare bondage has left the Negro male in the slum with few other options than a smouldering resentment and fantasies of dominance and destruction as a source of self-esteem.[2] There are many sources to the exhilaration seen and heard from the rioters during a ghetto uprising, but a major one is the sense of importance that derives from it. Suddenly Watts and Hough become known throughout the world. "Now you see us, Whitey, and tremble."

The concept of "Black Power" and "Black Nationalism" have captured the imagination and loyalty of many Negroes not by talking of his problems but by appealing to his pride. Now one hears the word "Black" not as a term of opprobrium, rejection, disgust, or indifference, but as something positive, strong, beautiful, and "soul"-ful. One hears in the ghettos a distinction between the "Black community" and the "Negro community," the latter referring to those who still aspire to making it within the white power structure. To the militants and the separatists, the word "Negro" carries a negative and self-effacing connotation. The very softness and openness of the word offends them—it is a word that seeks nonexistence—one can vocalize it without moving the lips. But "Black" comes on strong, hard, abruptly. It cannot be mumbled or misunderstood, and the affective ripples which surround it are not muted.

No greater violence can be done to a person or a group than to destroy its pride. I have rarely seen a more poignant illustration of the deficiencies of self-esteem in the American Negro than in the studies of the psychologist Kenneth Clark. He found that five year old Negro children

preferred to play with white dolls and persistently de-
meaned Negro dolls. They were demeaning themselves,
and at five years of age, that was their self-image.

Police brutalities against urban Negroes are no myth.
They exist and are widespread. But what exists far more
pervasively, systematically, openly, and destructively are
police indignities. A middle-class white man who drives
through a stop sign will be stopped by a police officer,
given a ticket, and perhaps even a tongue-lashing, and we
know what frustration and annoyance that provokes. If
we are with our wife or a date, it is humiliating. But
imagine what our feeling would be if after being stopped
we were pulled out of the car, spread-eagled, and searched.
The Negro who goes through a stop sign frequently has
that happen to him. I need hardly mention the added insult of a grown man's being called "Boy."

From a legal point of view there is a great difference
between brutality and insult. But if we do not recognize
that indignities can be brutal, that psychological assaults
can be as painful and destructive as physical ones, we will
continue to provoke bitterness, resentment, and uncompromising hostility.

Unfortunately, the white liberal, because of his very
desire to be helpful, must assume some responsibility for
the psychological damage done to the urban Negro. Try
to recall when during a time of defeat, failure and helplessness, a person, otherwise equal to you but stronger, more
resourceful, or more secure, came to your aid. He may
have protected you, or guided you, or saved your life.
Along with the feeling of gratitude, can you remember a
dim, uncomfortable resentment—unstated and barely recognized? Perhaps you can even recall a touch of hatred

towards the helper—because he was the one who saved you.

The most destructive thing in psychotherapy is a "rescue fantasy" in the therapist—a feeling that the therapist is the divinely sent agent to pull a tormented soul from the pit of suffering and adversity and put him back on the road to happiness and glory. A major reason this fantasy is so destructive is that it carries the conviction that the patient will be saved only through and by the therapist. When such a conviction is communicated to the patient, verbally or otherwise, he has no choice other than to rebel and leave or become even more helpless, dependent, and sick.

The intensity of feeling behind the Black Power movement is not just hostility and distrust of the white man, though that too is there. It is primarily a desperate need to feel that the Negro can fight his own battles and not be dependent upon the good will of the white man.

When Stokeley Carmichael says that the activist white liberal should go organize the poor whites in Appalachia, he is not, after all, telling him to go to Hell. The suggestion is not a bad one, and the reluctance of the white college student to help people of his own race suggests something unpalatable about his motivation to help Negroes. The same unpalatable quality emerges from the sudden hostility of the white liberal when confronted with Black Nationalism. What is unpalatable is the possibility that the motivation to help the Negro was predicated on the Negro's remaining helpless; that the sense of satisfaction, of enhanced self-esteem, of nobility within the liberal was earned through exploitation. I am saying that the white liberal can exploit the Negro *for the white liberal's own salvation.*

Sometimes we have to see things in a displaced form or as a parable before the true meaning can be assimilated. I never fully recognized the impact of these thoughts until I read the novel *Resurrection* by Leo Tolstoy.[3]

The story opens as a charming, witty, and handsome prince rises in the morning and, with great satisfaction, bathes, grooms, and dresses himself. He is completely pleased with his life as he thinks of his passionate mistress who will soon be replaced by a lovely and aristocratic wife.

One of the reasons he is so pleased with himself is that he anticipates performing a civil obligation to serve on a jury. He was idealistic as a youth, having even toyed with ideas of socialism and land reform, but he is more mature now and all that remains is a sense of civic responsibility.

Seated in the jury box, he is confronted with the criminal, a prostitute accused of murder. With a shock of recognition he remembers her as the first girl he ever seduced. She was a maid in his aunt's house ten years before, and he, then a student, fell in love with her. They lost their innocence together, and she became pregnant. He left to further his brilliant career and closed his soul to tender feelings, and she began her downward spiral until now, as a prematurely aged whore accused of murder and robbery, she stands before her ex-lover.

The prince's soul is ripped open by the revelation of her disintegration and its source in him. Throughout the proceedings he is agonized by the growing shame and remorse in his breast. The woman is found guilty and he walks dazed through the remainder of his daytime activities. The hypocrisy and emptiness of his life confronts him everywhere. The day ends in his garden where in an intense conversion experience he resolves to give up the trappings of his superficial and hedonistic existence, to give away his wealth, to go to the miserable and forelorn creature who was once young and beautiful, to marry her and spend his life with her in Siberia if her innocence cannot be proven.

He is overwhelmed with joy and falls into a sound sleep. The next day with his heart full and his eyes wet he goes to her in prison, identifies himself, and on his knees asks her, the doomed whore, to marry him, the repentant prince.

His reawakened idealism has yet another shock, however. With a slight and seductive smile his redeemer says, "I don't want to marry you, but do you have ten rubles?"

The prince had one more revelation to make, not in a garden with joy bursting in his heart, but on a dusty road winding toward a flat horizon, with a weary wisdom in his heart. His first conversion was not a conversion at all but only a narcissistic reshuffle. The girl was still his instrument, this time not for his lust, but for his salvation. And the girl knew it.

And the inner-city Negro knows it when the Great White Liberals come to him with their open minds and open smiles and open hands. They just don't understand. It isn't only that three hundred years of deprivation and deceit are unlikely to be erased by an offer of friendship but also that the offer of friendship is itself so self-conscious and self-satisfied as to be offensive.

To turn suddenly illiberal and wish for the defeat of more militant Negro activists is never to have wanted their success in the first place. A truly liberal response to the Black Power movement might be to express a wish for success without the shedding of blood. One might also, like the psychiatrist to the departing patient, merely remind the recipient of help that the helper will still be around to give assistance in the future if more is needed.

Integration may have been one of our cherished visions. But if it is seen by Negroes as an imposition of white, middle-class, liberal prejudice on their own desires for independent comfort, for good education, gratifying employment and rat-free homes, then there is too high a price to pay for insisting on it. The price is the loss of their self-esteem in our insisting that they do it our way if the crimes done to them are to be undone.

What arrogance, to expect the whore gratefully to marry the prince who caused her downfall just because he now wants to undo his crime.

The third inner-city deficit that provokes rioting and that rioting serves to correct is a *sense of community*. Men need to relate, and they need to feel that their relationships are meaningful.

That man is in fact a gregarious animal and requires contact with other human beings hardly requires psychiatric substantiation. Throughout our history we have seen how social isolation and solitary confinement have been among the most intolerable conditions known to man. In his book *Alone*,[4] Admiral Byrd described the torment of his self-imposed isolation at the South Pole. He concluded that a man cannot do without sounds, smells, voices and touch any more than he can do without calcium and phosphorous.

The real life person on whom the story of *Robinson Crusoe* was based did not fare very well after his years of isolation. When he returned to England, he was a highly suspicious and disagreeable person and eventually lived out his life as a recluse within civilization.

It is not, however, enough that human beings be near other human beings. There must be a meaningful relationship between them. A great deal has already been said of "lonely crowds" and "anomie."

On a broader and more significant scale, Alexander Leighton demonstrated the direct relationship between disintegrated, unorganized communities and rates of mental illness. (Chapter I, reference 1.)

As another instance of the importance of the nature of communal life to individual behavior, there were observations of the Puerto Rican slum-dwellers who were moved from decrepit shacks to clean, modern, high-rise "caseiros."[5] Large numbers of the people who made this move were very unhappy, bickered with their neighbors, and frequently expressed a nostalgic longing for the old slum. What was ignored in the design of a more wholesome environment was the need the people had to engage in conversations in small communal spaces, to have constant, informal interactions. The essence of their communal life, which had gratifications as well as deprivations and frustrations, was lost.

Still another example of the importance of a sense of community is the study of the West End in Boston.[6] A cohesive but culturally variegated and lively neighborhood was totally destroyed in an early and improvident urban renewal program. Studies of the relocated population showed heightened incidences of mental hospitalization after moving. Particularly striking was a widespread reaction of grief for their lost neighborhood; the reaction was indistinguishable from a clinical depression.

A ghetto is not a community. The forces which tie people together and provide them with a sense of common purpose, identity, or direction do not arise simply because people are forced by segregation and poverty to live together. Recent migrants to northern ghettos from the rural South frequently report that they felt closer and more friendly towards the much more distant neighbors they had in the South then they now feel in the densely packed northern slum.

This changes during a riot, however. As when any common enemy appears on the horizon or during any period of crisis or disaster, a spontaneous mobilization of group resources, a sense of commonality, mutuality, and camaraderie emerges; in short, a sense of community develops. This experience was evident among the usually anomic, disintegrated masses in the Northeast Corridor during the power blackout of 1966. The presence of universal anxiety and a strange and novel experience seemed to knit together this urban mass.

A more striking example of the power of a crisis situation to bring people together occurred at the time of President Kennedy's assassination. It was as if the entire country, perhaps the world, had for a moment become less fragmented, had a tragically beautiful taste of universal brotherhood in the state of common grief. Even schizophrenics, lost to one another through primitive narcissism and autism, could develop some sense of group identity during the experience of common and intense loss.[7]

It is the quality of a common destiny, of unity, that develops in a ghetto during a riot. It is the Black People of Watts or Hough or North Philadelphia or Newark against the police and the white man. It is a highly expensive and destructive form of community organization but it is nonetheless a constructive phenomenon inasmuch as it creates a sense of community.

The fourth major deficit feeding into the symptomatology of urban violence is that of a sense of *environmental mastery*: control over one's environment and of one's own destiny. If the line between the individual and his environment is a fluid and arbitrary one, if the individual is, at least in part, defined by his environment, then the extent to which a person can influence his environment will determine his ability to perceive himself as a separate human being. If the infant remained completely dependent upon and responsive to environmental stimuli, it is unlikely that he would ever perceive himself as distinct from everything about him. He learns within the first three or four months of life that if he emits certain sounds he will be fed or changed or held. He learns that some of his facial grimaces consistently elicit expressions of warmth and love from the face of that nurturer-giantess above him who is so inconstantly present. Perhaps it is not her inconstancy that permits the infant to recognize that his mother is not a part of him, but rather the fact that at times he can make her smile.

We must learn that the environment is responsive to us, that some part of the cosmos, however small, yields to our touch, is beckoned by our will or is shaped by our hand. If we do not learn this at all, we carry the burden of a severe emotional disability. If we learn it inadequately or out of scale, we may have difficulty in mastering our own impulses or we may become preoccupied with a will to power, a need to control others that will dominate our lives as well as the lives of our victims. If we do learn this lesson well and in proper scale and then are thrust into an environment which is no longer responsive to us, we become enraged.

Can you remember a feeling of anger during a group discussion when every time you made a statement you were interrupted or ignored? Try to imagine what it would be like if you found yourself in a dreamlike world in which your very existence was not acknowledged, in which people looked through you rather than at you, in which they didn't seem to hear your voice or feel your touch. Remember Yank in O'Neill's play, *The Hairy Ape*, shouting with rage at the sedate, preoccupied women and gentlemen on Fifth Avenue who acted as if he were not there? And the next time you have the opportunity of watching a derelict begging for money, look for the ways he reacts to the man who rudely waves him away and to the more sensitive person who walks on pretending he has not noticed the panhandler. It is the latter person who gets the mumbled obscenity. We would rather be hated than ignored. This is true of everyone except the most disturbed schizophrenics on the chronic wards of mental hospitals who protect themselves from everything, including kindness, as if everything were an assault.

The need to feel some control over the environment, to leave a fleeting imprint of one's foot or hand or soul on the matrix of the world is a basic psychological need and the frustration of that need can wreak havoc.

The impoverished Negro in the northern ghetto can only react passively and helplessly to the exploitative or bureaucratic institutions that channel his behavior. The police, the schools, the welfare system, the employment system, the credit system have boxed him in. All around him is the rhetoric and image of a democratic society, but in practice it is only the privileged who are *served* by this society's institutions. The underprivileged are *commanded* by these institutions out of paternalism, distrust, or greed.

The dyssocial method of exercising power is, of course, through brute force and violence as during a riot,[8] but how can an individual exert power and control in a way that is undestructive and sanctioned by the laws and standards of the Nation? In two forms is the exercise of power acceptable—through politics and through economics.

It was a dream of the civil rights movement that with expanded voter registration among Negroes and with emerging Negro majorities in the cities, that political power would finally devolve upon the Negro poor. The image of the great political machines, the patronage, the kingmaking, the underground empires that city hall summons up seemed to provide a significant and realizable promise of the emergence of the Negro as a force in American life.

Power, however, does not change hands quite so smoothly. In one city close to having a Negro majority and eventually a Negro mayor, the incumbent political machine is quietly, gradually, and relentlessly giving tenure to the current appointed officials. When the first Black mayor appears on that scene, he will be confronted with a pseudomorph of political power, having no patronage to dispense.

In other areas, there is talk of and in some cases planning for metropolitan government, incorporating the central city and its suburbs into a single administrative unit. While some of us would praise such a move as a step in the direction of integrated planning, equilibration of the tax base, and racial and economic desegregation, let us not have any illusions about the motives behind a sudden interest in metro-government. It is a method of keeping city hall in the hands of the white, middle class which has already fled to the suburbs.

Whether or not metropolitan government or the control of patronage effectively limits the political power of the inner-city Negro, there is little question that the administrative unit he may win will be financially bankrupt. With the highly taxable middle-class resident as well as a good deal of industry fleeing the core-city like some kind of cosmic explosion, with the continued in-migration of unemployed and unemployable Negro poor relying upon welfare for their subsistence, it is not a very sound business that will be won by the Negroes in City Hall.

There is finally a much more subtle and more devastating problem attendant upon the Negro's assumption of political control in the city. Political power in the city is being redefined.

A wholly new urban professional is being spawned from the universities. Social policy planners rather than brick and mortar city planners are being developed. These are people whose training is in sociology, anthropology, criminology, political science, and mental health as well as in architecture and urban design. Systems analysts from large and sophisticated organizations capable of developing elaborate defense systems or sending missiles into space are turning their attention to air pollution, traffic patterns, solid waste disposal and the delivery of social services.

Professor Donald Michael[9] has been pointing out

that incumbent politicians are recognizing their inability to solve urban problems in the old ad hoc way, responding to immediate problems as manifested by vested interests. Decision making is becoming more integrated, scientific, rationalized, professionalized, and long range in its perspectives. Simulation models, gaming techniques, program budgeting, and systems analysis are being looked to to deal with the structural and social problems choking the cities.

This is fine, except that long-range planning effectively disenfranchises a community because the polity being planned for does not yet exist. By the time the urban Negro can win control of the city, control will no longer reside in the old kind of political clout but with the professionals, the planners, the computer experts who make up a technological elite, whose methods are so complex as to be esoteric. Professor Michael sees their decision making as tantamount to *arcana imperii*—secret remedies for public ills. Apart from the implications of this to American democracy, the impact on the Negro will be profound. He will find himself once again deferring to the white middle class. He is going to feel tricked by an establishment that has redefined and emasculated power just prior to giving it up.

The urban Negro will face a number of frustrations, then, if his need for environmental mastery is to rely entirely on the expression of political power. But we have known for a long time that economic power is every bit as effective as political power in controlling the environment. There are, moreover, reasons to believe that what passes as political power in this country is very often a thinly disguised expression of the pre-potency of money.

The official and respectable reference to economic power in the ghetto is in terms of employment. Give the Negroes jobs in American business is the pious plea, get them off the streets, get them off welfare, let them contribute to the American economy as they climb their personal ladders of success. What the Negro needs, continues this sermon, is a bit of the Horatio Alger mystique, industriousness, resourcefulness, ambition—the baptism by the American Dream.

This is a myth. It is a delusion on the part of those who have won success to calm momentarily their anxiety or to assuage their guilt. The majority of ghetto Negroes, particularly the young men, cannot get on even the first rung of the ladder because of arrest records (of which it is difficult to be free in the ghetto), because of inadequate education (even a high school diploma from a ghetto does not mean literacy), because of qualifying tests which exclude them (I.Q. tests are not a measure of the intelligence of the Negro), and because, still, of overt discrimination.

If the Negro does reach the first rung of the ladder, he soon finds that the ladder is based in quicksand so that every rise in the organization, in his status, or income is only an apparent one. Under current circumstances, the lower-class Negro has very few employment options other than the most menial and poorly paying jobs offering no opportunity for advancement. This is why the pious sermon has been expanded to include training and education for new kinds of jobs. But there may be a deception here too. If the *rate* of automation continues as it has been, there will come a time during the next generation when inconceivable numbers of jobs will be obsolete.[10] Many of these will be precisely the jobs for which the urban Negro received training.

Job training and education for future employment are not only long-term investments but, also, the payoff even in the long run may be very small. As long, however, as we are dominated by the Protestant ethic, as long as a dole is stigmatized as something shameful, as long as we expect that a consumer must also be a producer, we will have to talk about employment, education, and job training. But let us remember that the end result in terms of power is money. There is a sense of control, fulfillment, and immediacy that comes from having the dollars in your pocket. No matter how depleted your ego resources and social skills, with money you are a master. This has probably always been true, but it is particularly true today in this country. Money is sacred, and we celebrate it with reverence and abandon. It isn't really so awful that we forgive villainy if it results in extraordinary wealth. What is horrifying is that we find the most dull, fatuous, and insipid people fascinating when they command great wealth. We love money with an intensity that used to be considered reserved to the sexual glands. The fact that the political scandals in this country invariably involve money and not sex suggests where our real interests are.

In this atmosphere of hypomanic ecstasy about what money can do, we expect welfare recipients to be saintly Calvinists concerned only with food, clothing, and shelter. They, because of their economic dependence on us, should be able to transcend our profligate greed, and their wanting T.V. sets and cars is offensive; yet ours is more than

respectable, it is a solemn obligation. We talk about crime
in the streets as if it were a cancer when it is actually a
metastasis from a malignancy much more deeply buried
in middle-class society. We are upset by looting during a
riot, as if a riot should be a liberal protest demonstration!
A riot is a violent expression of a basic need; the need for
the trivia that the whole world is knocking itself out trying to get is as basic as any other. It is no accident that
the National Guard comes in with its cannons and tanks
when looting starts. We are most intolerant in others of
the shameful tendencies we barely recognize in ourselves.

Ever since man found himself in the business of creating values, there has been a current of consciousness
about the true meaning of money. Rarely with reverence,
occasionally with respect, but most often with cynicism
or outright contempt, have we recognized the voices within and outside of us that decry the bitch goddess. The
few who have sought to enrich mankind with their own
revelations about love, wisdom, or art as more constant
sources of happiness than money have always been disap-
pointed. They have found mankind unwilling to listen
or, if listening, unwilling to believe that money is not the
very stuff of life, the reason for our existence. And all too
often, the idealists themselves have fallen under the spell
of money. All the pleasures and mysteries of nature and
man's universe are promised with wealth, great wealth,
inconceivable wealth. Like a skin lesion that itches more
the more it is scratched, the accumulation of money never
reaches a point of climax or even of quiet fulfillment. But
it brings the person one unquestionable distinction, the
absence of poverty. And as Lear's jester says, "Fortune,
the arrant whore, never turns the key to the poor."

There may come a time when the world will be shaken by a compassionate revolution and the yoke of the bitch goddess finally broken, when beauty and the capacity for love and excellence of spirit in forms not yet imagined will be the mark of a man rather than the gold he commands. But that time is not yet. As long as there are rich people and poor people, materialism will dominate the world. You cannot tell a poor man that what he dreams of and has never tasted is not worth having. And you cannot tell a rich man that what he has devoted his life to obtaining and what everyone else covets is not worth keeping.

When the distinction between the rich and the poor is gone, when the arrogance and power of wealth and the hunger and helplessness of poverty no longer exist, then man may begin to find out what life is all about.

> The young man saith unto him, All these things have I kept from my youth up: what lack I yet?
>
> Jesus said unto him, If thou wilt be perfect, go and sell that thou hast, and give to the poor, and thou shalt have treasure in heaven: and come and follow me.
>
> But when the young man heard that saying, he went away sorrowful: for he had great possessions.

This, then, is the diagnosis. A riot is a symptomatic expression of deficits of stimulation, self-esteem, a sense of community, and environmental mastery. The treatment of the condition is no secret and in inadequate dosages it has already been administered. The problem is that inadequate treatment can be worse than no treatment at all. Physicians are encountering the phenomenon of iatrogenic illness more and more. Iatrogenic disease merely refers to the disorders that physicians themselves have induced. Antibiotic-resistant infections, drug reactions, and complications of surgery are such examples. There are analogues in the urban condition. An improvident urban renewal program, the frustrations of unkept promises, the provocations of overly aggressive police practices, and the resentment following condescending and ineffectual gestures (like plastic swimming pools) serve to aggravate problems rather than palliate them.

We have seen the incredibly sad picture of the urban therapists themselves forgetting their superordinate goal, the well-being of their patients, in their endless arguing about how and where to administer treatment.[11]

It tragically happens in medicine that institutional or specialty loyalties or an inordinate investment in a favored treatment prevents physicians from working together, putting the patient in the difficult position of having to choose between expert opinions. This frequently results in an irrational choice or a distrust of all "expert" opinion.

The urban "experts," particularly those addressing themselves to the issue of race relations, are practically at each other's throats about whether integrated schools are better than superior Negro schools, about whether cultural deprivation or broken families or segregation is most responsible for the Negro's problems, about whether money should be spent in schools or family allowances or case services. We have seen the absurd and tragic scene of having people of goodwill and basic agreement call each other "racist" because of semantic or highly theoretical differences. It would be as if a patient were to die of a strep infection because physicians were so occupied in argument as to whether penicillin should be given orally or intra-muscularly that none was given at all.

This is not the time for the "narcissism of small differences." We ought to be grateful for the opportunity for taking a pluralistic approach to the problem. Instead of breaking up into parochial camps and making fortresses out of them, we might be applying every reasonable approach in a great natural experiment.

Integration and "golden ghettos" are mutually exclusive only if they are seen as total programs, beautiful and true now and forevermore. Life and social change are not like that. Both approaches have advantages and drawbacks, and, probably, different groups will respond in different ways.

It is too easy to stereotype inner-city Negroes as a homogenous group with a single array of aspirations. The reality is that there are sharp distinctions along class and generational lines. The upwardly mobile, middle-class Negro, accustomed to an urbanized industrial environment, values integration much more than does the recent in-migrant caught in a web of unemployability and alienation. To the latter, a program of vitalizing the ghetto with jobs, Negro-owned businesses, adequate low-cost housing, and excellent schools is far more important.

If we are concerned with freedom (mental health), then we want to structure an environment with the widest possible options. A program of social change which is monolithic and restrictive will not have that result. Integration must be offered the Black Man, along with the option of turning it down.

The treatment of sick organisms does not always result in immediate or even gradual improvement. In medicine, surgery, and psychotherapy, the treatment itself frequently causes an exacerbation of the patient's condition. In the effort to correct a disorder, surgery can be a dangerous and occasionally fatal assault on the body. In the postencephalitic behavior disorder of children, the specific treatment, amphetamine drugs, frequently causes a temporary worsening of the condition before it results in an improvement. In psychotherapy it is not unusual for anxiety to be deliberately stimulated so that further work can be done.

The fact that cities continue to have riots even in the face of attempts to meet the social needs of their ghettos should not mean that those attempts are in vain. That relatively competent and progressive cities have had riots does not mean that they were going in the wrong direction. In the same vein, the very fact that the years of urban violence follow so closely the years of the civil rights movement and antipoverty legislation does not mean that those forces were pathogenic. The stimulation of hope like the draining of an abscess may cause an ugly, if temporary, state of being. De Tocqueville, in writing about the French Revolution, said, "The French found their position intolerable when it had become better. . . . The evil, which was suffered patiently as inevitable, seems unendurable as soon as the idea of escaping from it is conceived."

You are entitled to ask a physician for a prognosis. I am not optimistic. I see no indication that the institutions of government in this country are capable of radical change. There is rhetoric and there is power, but the rhetoric is empty of ideology and the power is directionless.

There are waves of reaction, containment, and authoritarianism that grow stronger and wider after each riot. Everywhere there are guns, hand weapons, shotguns, automatic weapons being sold to black and white alike, the final integrationist being death.

The cities will become blacker and poorer and the surrounding middle-class white suburbs more distant. The area between the haves and the have-nots will widen rather than narrow and will be across a gray area of constant violence. Each family will have its own weapons, curfews will be enforced throughout the year and the National Guard will be in unending attendance. In its response to urban violence, the Nation will learn to ignore the first ten amendments of the Constitution.

Demands for political power by the unaffiliated, unskilled poor will become more urgent, while those in command of that power will find themselves unable to muster the planning, sophistication and resources to solve the grossest urban problems.

Metropolitan America will be a segregated garrison state, choked with violence, pollution, and congestion and paralyzed by an uncoordinated and fragmented power base. In the face of endless death and destruction, with violence interjecting itself regularly into our lives, we will retreat from the streets in terror. We will seek security and safety and turn to promises of uncompromising strength and order from our leaders. Liberals will be ridiculed and finally persecuted. American democracy will die.[12]

With the talents and resources of the richest nation in the world dissipated and preoccupied with internal conflict, the populations of Asia, Africa, and South America will continue to grow and continue to starve. Before a massive depopulation of the world caused by disease and starvation, the billions of desperately hungry people will no longer be able to tolerate the showplace existence of Western prosperity. Europe and North America will be surrounded and finally engulfed by a sea of humanity. In the brute struggle for existence, civilization itself will perish. In the end, Nature, blind, indifferent, unloving, will attempt to restore the world to some kind of ecological balance, and man will no longer be the measure of things.

This is the grim prognosis held out to us by an extrapolation of present trends. Of course, linear extrapolations are unreasonable and it is entirely likely that some combination of rational and irrational forces will provide some hope. But in the past we had time to play with and to feed hope with while now time has become our enemy.

Those in the mental health professions who consider social change irrelevant to their practice might give some thought to what the role of psychotherapy will be when human life becomes a struggle for survival once again. Or they might seek ways in which they could encourage and participate in the critical retooling of American institutions.

In the past, social change was a luxuriant fantasy of man's social conscience. Since the 18th Century, Western man harbored a faith in progress, a faith in his own capacity to improve his lot. There was a feeling of a job to be done—a bridge to be built to a life of freedom and opportunity in which poverty and war and sickness would exist no longer. The feeling existed and has persisted throughout socialism, Marxism, the New Deal, and even, God help us, the Great Society, that at some point we will mobilize our resources and make life better.

Social change, however, has become a different kind

of animal. We have reached a period in history when it is no longer a matter of *progress* but a matter of *survival*. If the institutions of government in this country cannot undergo the revolutionary-like changes that are required by contemporary needs while maintaining the structure of democracy, the needs will not be met and the death of democracy will accompany the frustrations of those needs.

In short, the changes I am talking about, the treatment for this ailing organism, involves a redistribution of the wealth and resources of this country on a scale that has never been imagined.

We should be constructing a society for the urban poor of such beauty and richness, with so many options for behavior, that it becomes nothing less than a privilege to be called poor. The schools and hospitals in the ghettos should be *better* than those in the suburbs. The mechanisms for participating in government should be *more effective* for the poor than for the affluent.

The gap between the haves and the have-nots in this country should be closed so quickly that for a while it would seem to be reversed. When this has happened, the Nation should direct its energies and resources and wealth to doing the same job for the rest of the world. There is only one rational way of responding to a revolution of rising expectations; outstrip them.

Psychiatrists have the rare capacity to see a problem as the resultant of dynamic forces. They are taught to see violent outbursts as expressions of pain and as cries for help rather than as viciousness and evil. They can bring to bear on a problem the skills and insights of biology, psychology and social science. They function at the interface between individual behavior and environmental forces. They carry the life and death responsibility and commitment of the physician.

We are dealing here with a pathological system. The frustration of basic needs in the face of rising expectations is being expressed in civil disorder. The disorder is being escalated to the point of civil war by an even more violent response of panic-ridden conservatism. There is a terrifying synergism between the war mentality engendered by our foreign policy and the polarization in our cities. The result of that synergism is a hardening of the lines between the haves and the have-nots, between the whites and the colored throughout the world. This is happening at a time when world population is growing and food production diminishing so rapidly that survival of the human species is threatened.

And in the cities, psychiatrists are doing little more than psychotherapy.

THE BAPTISM BY BEER

5

To learn surgery without operating or anatomy without dissecting a cadaver is not possible. Nor is it possible to learn how to do psychotherapy without doing psychotherapy. For skills and sophistication to be developed, there has to be a direct exposure to the subject matter.

The community psychiatrist who relies on theoretical or indirect knowledge about the community is like the medical student who does a "dry dissection" (the student who learns all his anatomy from textbook illustrations rather than the cadaver dissection); he knows the vocabulary but does not know how to recognize in reality what he knows by written instruction must be there.

If the psychiatrist is going to talk about the community, he must be exposed to it. One such exposure in my own experience was in an urban renewal area and I focused my observations on homeless men.

Homeless men cling to the underside of every major city.[1] Their presence rarely intrudes on the individual and group forces that dominate urban life. When some of their unkempt or intoxicated members penetrate the more respectable downtown areas, they are given a wide berth by citizens and an aggressive scrutiny by the police. Their maintenance is the unwilling responsibility of public welfare departments, and their medical care is perfunctorily administered in the emergency wards of public hospitals.[2]

They are looked upon as a parasitic blight on cities, as social outcasts whose misery is self-imposed, or, at best, they are tolerated as men of no importance. Their communities are the prime targets of urban renewal forces and rarely is their future whereabouts the consideration of even the most social minded city planners.

Through what agency can a community psychiatrist approach this population? In what institution do these men congregate willingly and openly and frequently enough for study and intervention to be feasible? A glance at their community will provide an answer, the tavern.

The Star Tavern is in the shadow of an elevated railroad in an area soon to be demolished by an urban renewal program. It is no escapist cocktail lounge with indirect lighting on tiers of delicate and expensive liquors. It is a typical lower class tavern[3] with large bottles of third-rate whisky and brandy, illuminated beer displays, unstable stools, and a bar that is a mosaic of stains and cigarette burns.

The barroom is almost never empty. In fact there

are usually two or three men waiting for it to be opened at 8 a.m. and a larger group having to be hurried out at midnight when it is closed for the night.

Rather than elaborate a strained approximation of naturalistic observations, I decided simply to show up at the tavern one morning, introduce myself to the bartender as a physician working at a nearby health unit, order a beer, and proceed to watch and listen.

Over a period of six months I returned to the tavern at varying times of the day once or twice a week and stayed about an hour on each occasion.

I rarely initiated conversation but responded amiably to greetings or comments when they were offered. The bartender, Peter, was open and convivial throughout. He seemed pleased at the presence and interest of this unusual patron and talked freely to me.

On one occasion I accepted an invitation to Peter's house and this seemed to enhance further the communication and mutual regard. I never identified myself to Peter as a psychiatrist, and though I was explicit about my interest in the health and life of his patrons, I did not indicate that I was engaged in any kind of study.

Peter has worked in the Star Tavern for fifteen years. For the same period he has owned a building two houses away in which ten rooms are let to men at a cost of six to nine dollars a week. Peter, who is a bachelor, lives in a two-room apartment in his house. His lodgers make up the main contingent of regulars in the tavern.

Peter is 64 years old. He was born in a rural village in Ireland, and though he has lived in this country for nearly half a century, he still speaks with a heavy brogue.

His community is predominantly Irish, so it is not difficult for old country habits to be maintained.

He is well liked by his lodgers and bar patrons. Most
of his lodgers have been with him for several years, and
they invariably pay their weekly rent promptly. It is, in
fact, standard for the "old-timers" to have their welfare
checks sent directly to the bar where Peter will deduct
his rent and bar bill and dispense the remainder to his
lodger.

He does not often socialize with the men in his room-
ing house, and except when they are acutely ill and require
hospitalization he leaves them alone. He strictly prohibits
cooking in the rooms but drinking is, of course, permitted.

Peter himself drinks moderately (two or three high-
balls a day) and though he permits the endless drinking in
his house and serves liquor in the bar, he is extremely
moralistic and constantly berates his regulars for their destructive drinking. At the same time that he serves liquor,
he will make references to "alcoholics killing themselves
with booze," or to "the old-timers' hanging around a stuffy
barroom all day" or to "the fact that liquor doesn't keep
you warmer in the cold weather."

These remarks, frequent as they are, do not seem to
annoy or antagonize his regulars. One wonders if these
contradictory messages from Peter reverberate with earlier
parental miscommunications and hostile-dependent relationships which may have played a role in their fate as
homeless men and alcoholics.

Peter, like most bartenders in lower class taverns, does
not belong to the bartender's union. This is because the
union is dominated by hotel and restaurant people who

depend heavily on tips. The union, according to Peter, prefers tipping to decent salaries because cocktail lounge bartenders can make considerably more money that way. In taverns like the Star, tipping is extremely uncommon.

The Star is owned by a man who operates three other similar taverns. Peter, who alternates with the owner's son in tending the bar, usually works from 8 a.m. to 4 p.m., the shift that caters to the homeless men in the area. After 4 p.m., the working men begin to filter in for their before-dinner drinks. By 6 p.m. this younger crowd, family men, dominates the bar, and the homeless lodgers who have been plateau drinking throughout the day have left and usually returned to their rooms.

According to the popular myth, the bartender is a patient and non-directive listener to whom patrons may pour out their stories. This is not the case with Peter. Indeed, the amount of his attention that a patron may command is carefully prescribed by the culture of the barroom.

Two groups of drinkers will be "shut out", i.e., not served. They are the "fighters" and the "pests". It is clear why the fighters will not be tolerated. This is a stable and conservative environment, and physical abuse or destructiveness is too threatening to a social system which must remain predictable and controlled to satisfy the needs of the regulars.

The "pest" or the "earbender" is the person who actually attempts to dominate Peter's attention. It does not refer to the patron who wishes to talk to other patrons as there is no apparent limit to that kind of discussion. It is quite specifically talk directed toward the bartender that is rationed. It is not only Peter who is sensitive to violations of this unwritten rule, but also the drinkers themselves who complain about one of their members who is trying to draw Peter into a conversation.

Peter does indeed talk to the group but invariably on his own initiative. His explicit reason for this controlled involvement with the group is that he is too busy for an extended conversation. On the other hand, he has also indicated his discomfort with talk that is too laden with affect. On one occasion he indicated a man who had just lost his wife. When I asked if the man talked about it much at the bar, Peter shook his head and said, "He tries to but I ignore him or change the subject. I don't want him to get emotional here."

That this avoidance of personal involvement with the drinkers at the bar is in part a function of his role was suggested by an incident that took place one afternoon. A drinker was approaching the point of being a pest by addressing many of his remarks to Peter. Peter's displeasure was indicated by his refusal to respond even to direct questions, by turning his back on the man, and by interrupting him midsentence to say something to another drinker. Precisely at 4 p.m., Peter was relieved by the other bartender. He took off his apron, put on his hat, and sat down on our side of the bar to have a drink himself. He no sooner sat down then he bought a drink for the would-be pest and began to engage him in conversation.

Though his talk as a bartender may be carefully limited in amount and nature, Peter can still be supportive. One of the several regulars whom I have identified as being psychotic said to an adjacent listener and within earshot of Peter that he had lost his job as a dishwasher because the Governor had discovered that he was on a secret mission for the F.B.I. Peter ignored the paranoid content of this communication and simply asked the man if he had applied for unemployment compensation. When he replied that he had not, Peter gave him directions to the appropriate office and urged him to get down there.

Peter is highly esteemed by the regulars, and their reasons for this esteem are that "He will not strong-arm you if you're drunk and act up," "He lends money if you're broke," and "He knows how much you should drink." It is clear that his firmness is a major reason for their respect. All the regulars know that once you have been shut out by Peter, you stay shut out "forever."

That he is indeed popular among the men is indicated by the observation that the only times the bar is empty is when he has a day off.

At any time between 8 a.m. and 4 p.m. there will be about ten men at the Star Tavern. This is the hard-core group of regulars who spend most of their daylight time in the bar. Their average age is sixty years, and they have the unkempt demeanor and haggard look that mark the homeless, unemployed, alcoholic population that counts them as members.

Their hours in the barroom are virtually obligatory in that during the winter, at least, they literally have no place else to go. Their rooms are frequently unheated, and in this area there is no mission or Salvation Army post or public reading room that will provide them with a daytime shelter. During the summer, they may wander around the square or make their way to a park, but it is only in the barroom that they can freely commune with one another and not have to avoid the police.

A major provision of the bar is the unrestricted opportunity to urinate. When they are not in their rooms, these men, who often have urinary frequency from the combination of alcohol intake, prostatism and urinary tract infections, have little opportunity to empty their bladders. They do not have the license that more respectable looking people have to use gas station or restaurant washrooms. The old-timers are occasionally arrested for exposing themselves while attempting to urinate.

Their health is uniformly poor. Cirrhosis and tuberculosis are almost universal in this group and rarely does a winter go by without each of them being hospitalized for pneumonia. Diabetes mellitus, peptic ulcers and bronchial asthma are also common.

Being a deviant group, their tolerance to deviant behavior is high. At least three of the regulars have had repeated state hospitalizations. They are referred to as "off but harmless" by the others. One old man who is voluble about his paranoid ideas as referred to as "the Town Crier," and though the owner has objected to his noise, the men and Peter permit him to stay and often buy his drinks for him.

The lucky ones of the group are on medical disability or social security pensions. The remainder, the larger number, get by on general relief. This amounts to $15.60 per week, and with a minimum of $6.00 per week for a room, they have precious little for food, alcohol, and cigarettes. Their staple diet is coffee and doughnuts. They occasionally have a plate of soup, rarely a hot dog or hamburger. (One analysis of the hot dog and hamburgers served to such a group indicated that they are filled with cereal and do not provide a minimal requirement for protein.)

The "admission fee" in the Star is fifteen cents for a fifteen ounce glass of beer. Except for Peter's lodgers, who are a privileged group, a drinker who does not re-order within an hour may be asked to leave. This rarely happens because bar credit is easy to come by and it is the pattern for any patron with extra money to stake the less fortunate drinkers as needed. Also an occasional "live one" will come in and buy drinks for everyone. This pattern of sharing is so regular that expressions of gratitude are rarely offered.

An ounce-and-a-half shot of whisky with a beer chaser at thirty-five cents is the most popular drink. For the plateau drinkers who are short of money, a glass of wine with a beer chaser is common.

This is a cohesive group and it is rare for any of its members to have a severe alcohol withdrawal condition because he cannot afford a drink to "feed his nerves." Obviously, too, this requires a certain stability of drinking pattern so that an equilibrium will not be disrupted by a constantly increasing need for alcohol. Most of the men seemed to have established their own level of plateau drinking. I saw only one or two of them ever severely intoxicated.

The men usually wake at 6 a.m., and by the time they have dressed and gone to a lunchroom for their morning meal of coffee and doughnuts, they are ready to begin waiting for the tavern to open. They return to their rooms for a midday nap and have another meal or a short walk, but for hours at a time the tavern is home base. They spend about six hours a day there and they are usually in bed again by 7 p.m.

Their inadequate diet is not supplemented by the local center that supplies surplus food to welfare recipients because the food requires preparation and the men are not permitted to cook or store food in their rooms.

The Star is closed on Sundays along with package stores so that a certain amount of preparation for that hardest day of the week is necessary. Peter's lodgers usually pitch in for a couple of bottles of wine to help see them through the day.

Alcohol may be the most potent instrument of social communion known to mankind. Whatever might be said of the countless families, nervous systems, and lives it has devastated, there can be little argument against alcohol's tendency to mitigate the psychological and social forces that cause people to preserve their separateness, unique individuality, and loneliness.[4]

The regulars at the Star Tavern form a cohesive and durable social system. They are their own and their only reference group. They are almost universally alienated from their families. Except for occasional spurts of unskilled labor, they have no identity as part of a work force. Most importantly, they are a group without a future. Most of them have no idea what they will do or where they will go when their shabby rooms and the tavern itself fall to the bulldozer.

For these men the tavern provides the only opportunity for socialization. It is a distortion to say that they spend their days in the barroom only to drink.

Conversation is always going on in the tavern. There is a constant flow of talk that may start between two members, widen to include eight or ten men, and break down again to smaller groups. It is usually Peter who acts as the carrier of the thread of conversation as, while standing at one end of the bar, he interjects a comment directed to the far end stimulating a response at his end as well.

The themes of conversation are remarkably few though with endless variation. The hopelessness and helplessness of the men's appearance, drinking, diet, and excessive sleep is reflected in their talk. This is a chronically depressed group and characteristically their talk revolves around loss, illness, isolation, and death.

These are a few representative samples of their overheard conversations:

Don: Cancer is from too many cigarettes.

Jack: John Wayne smoked five packs a day, and they took a piece out of his lung.

Don: I just take a couple of drags from each butt.

Tom: I heard of a guy who got cirrhosis of the liver, and he never took a drink in his life.

Jack: Yeah, but most of it's from too much booze and no food.

Don: You get holes in your liver.

Larry: Remember Smitty? He was a nice guy.

Peter: He died in my place. He was sitting up in bed with his hat and coat on.

Dick: There's a wake now for Frank.

Peter: I guess I'll go.

Ed: They close those places at ten.

Peter: They used to stay open all night.

John: Remember the guy who used to drive that blue truck? He got cancer.

Dick: Once you got it, it's only a matter of time.

Steve: You live as long as your parents did. I'm due any time now.

Mike: After you're sixty it's downhill.

Ed: That hospital stinks. If you turn around for a
second they'll steal your cigarettes.
Don: And try to get a glass of water from a nurse.

Tom: I lost a thousand dollars in that fucking bank
down the street in the depression. The financial experts
didn't lose anything. They knew it was coming. The workers and longshoremen lost everything.

Dan: This neighborhood once had 35,000 people.
Now it's down to 18,000. Stores are closing all over with
the renewal.
Jack: This city is dying.

It was characteristic of the men to see urban renewal
there as a death of the city. It would, in fact, be the death
of their city.

Arguments were uncommon in the tavern. The men's
hostility was either internalized or focused on the establishment from which they were so alienated. The forces of
urban renewal, the police, and the welfare department
were, in particular, the targets of cynical contempt.

There was a color television set over the bar. It was
always turned on but it served more as a background stimulus than a center for attention. Peter once said, "If I
owned a bar I wouldn't have a T.V., just a radio. When
the set was broken, I was the only one who missed it.
The boys didn't care. Look at that, twelve men at the bar
and not one is watching it."

I did note one occasion when the television seemed

to play a central role in the group process. A fifteen-minute religious program was broadcast every morning. This consisted of a sermon by a different clergyman on each occasion and was usually ignored. One morning, however, a minister talked about lonely and isolated men. The substance of his talk was a detailed description of the film, *The Pawnbroker,* a story of an embittered man whose state of mind resulted from terrible concentration camp experiences. As the minister abstracted this story to the level of all alienated men, including deviants and alcoholics, he seemed to strike a chord in the Star Tavern. All conversation, drinking, and cigarette puffing stopped. The only sounds were the Reverend's voice and the husky breathing of these broken men. There was an air of a common destiny, of a tacit recognition of their shared misery that seemed intensely religious. It was a while before conversation began again. There was no reference to the sermon.

It is probably easier for a social scientist to engage in such a study than a physician. During and after my encounters with the tavern, I found myself thinking of unmet needs and potential remedies rather than accuracy or generalizability.

As an indication of this, when I reached the point of feeling that I had observed enough of the culture of the Star to write a case study, I decided to shift roles and use my relationship with Peter to make an intervention. I convinced him to stock a supply of thiamine tablets and dispense one each day to those of his regulars whose diets were most deficient. I obtained the vitamins for him, and he began to give them out regularly.

Such issues as how to maintain this operation, how

to engage other agencies in it, and what its effects on the social system of the tavern might be are obviously matters for further study.

I suppose we have not yet reached the point when a barroom can be part of a network of health agencies. For many, the idea of using a bartender or his bar as a health and welfare resource may be construed as lending official sanction to a phenomenon that is ordinarily considered a social evil.

On the other hand, anyone who has attempted to deal with the emotional, physical, and social ailments of this population through traditional channels knows what a futile exercise it seems to be.

If we are actually to be concerned with the well-being of a population and not with the preservation of cherished institutional techniques, then uncomfortable innovations will have to be tried.

The barroom hangout of homeless men does not exist only to exploit and aggravate social pathology. It performs a life-sustaining function for men who have literally nothing else. It may provide their only opportunity for a tolerant and supportive environment, for socialization, for rest, and for warmth.

When urban designers reach the stage of planning for these men as well as for the more established poor, they will have much to learn from the taverns. In the meantime, those health professionals who already feel a responsibility to deal with the well-being of all people should not pass up the opportunity to use taverns as outposts.

THE PSYCHIATRIST AS CREATIVE ARTIST

6

People who have devoted their lives to mending the broken lives of others are engaged in a mysterious process. They plumb the depths of conflicted and unhappy souls, they look for the sources of conflict and misery within the individual, in his family, his institutions, his society, his culture, and finally in the human condition itself. They assume responsibility for resolving conflicts and assuaging psychic pain. They confront the tragic absurdity of human life with the baptized ignorance of science.

We would be so much happier if we could be more like technicians and less like philosophers. We look toward basic research as shipwrecked seamen toward solid land. Yet, what are we asking of research? To tell us what the meaning of life is, to tell us why some bits of a huge, disorganized, kaleidoscopic pattern of behavior and aspiration are more important, acceptable, or modifiable than others, and to do this with a dispassionate and value-free precision? How foolish we are to think that everything that is unknown can become known in the very same way —that ecstasy, dread and ennui, ideology, sacrifice and love will become less mysterious if analyzed by the same techniques used to analyze sound, light and gravity!

Do we really have to understand everything about our work to make it meaningful? Whether in psychoanalysis or social planning, does the psychiatrist really want as precise information about his subject or the process of working with it as the biochemist or physiologist? Well, of course he does! Who would turn his back on knowledge? Yet, while the artist may not turn away from knowledge about color and its perception nor the musician turn away from knowledge about the physical and physiological aspects of sound transmission, he knows how really irrelevant this knowledge is to the creation of a work of art. Perhaps in some respects, at some level, or at certain times, the psychiatrist shares something with the artist. He becomes the agent of forces that he does not understand and which he does not care to understand.

The Neanderthal who drew pictures on the walls of his cave when he might better have employed himself in the hunt with his brothers was partaking of something eternal. He was capturing the soul of his prey and partaking of the elements of faith. He must have suffered as every artist does.

That divine suffering has itself been the best grist for the artist's mill. Mann's Tonio Kröger comes to mind, doomed to look at life as through a pane of glass—or perhaps a better example is Fellini's film 8½. This film is a work of art that describes its own creation. We, the viewer, become the artist; we have no choice but to identify with the man as we see his dreams, memories, and fantasies and experience his reality. The camera is always on him or in him so that both his inner and outer world are experienced by us.

The artist is a film-maker who has taken his staff and equipment to a spa to recapture a lost inspiration or decide whether to finish his unstarted film. He awakens from a nightmare of bizarre death and judgment to confront doctors and nurses of the sanitarium and his very own Greek chorus, his co-writer who comments cynically and negatively about the meaninglessness of every event, thought, and recollection which the artist has had and has placed in his scenario. But with what incredible intensity and loving care is each experience drawn and the whole drawn together! The people seen, met, remembered are drawn with as much care and fascination as himself, his wife, his mistress, and his co-writer. Just as Rembrandt paints an old woman paring her nails with as much dignity as a duchess examining a jewel, every detail of warmth, humor, duplicity, jealousy, grief, and lust is portrayed as in itself a thing joyful to behold. After seeing the film, one can range over the film with one's memory picking out spots of exquisite perfection just as one points to a Cezanne orange or anticipates a movement of music within a favorite symphony: a dream of tearless sobbing at his father's funeral, a recollection of punishment because of boyhood sensuality and atonement before a seductively smiling madonna, an absurd mistress not loved but needed because she permits lovemaking to become a mise en scène. Such scenes are tied together into the film being made within the film being watched and the co-writer torments its creator by incessant reminders of the pointlessness of the scenes and their irrelevance to one another. But he is wrong.

Early in the story, the director attends an evening entertainment perfunctorily provided by the resort, and, after a decaying chanteuse (still fascinating despite her over-ripe voice and appearance), a mindreading act presents itself. The shadow of a formally attired man appears on a screen. The man suddenly bursts into laughter and appears in the flesh—part clown, part mystic, part actor in his make-up—and shouts, "Maya, let's entertain these bores." He walks from table to table pulling objects from the pockets or handbags of spectators while the blindfolded seer calls them out. He holds his hands over the heads of people; she calls out their thoughts. A borderline psychotic young woman becomes hysterical at the thought that her mind with its primitive contents will be read; she is comforted and led away by her companions. Wandering behind them is our director who greets the mindreader's consort as an old friend, then asks how it is done. He says with candor and a pleased simplicity that he doesn't know, but somehow when she is in the proper frame of mind, the objects he manipulates can be seen and interpreted by her. "Will she do it for me?" asks the director. With her agent's hands over his head, the mindreader laughs and writes down three meaningless words from the childhood of the director, and we are shown the scene of their origin—a creation of maternal love and childlike charm.

The mindreader does not appear again but her agent

does in the final scene, and his role becomes significant. After a crescendo of despair, frustration, and self-doubt, with fantasies of suicide and public mockery in his mind (the *paparazzi* of *La Dolce Vita* dance around him like flies), the director succumbs to the intellectual judgment of the co-writer and is about to drive off, abandoning the film, the actors, the props, everything. The co-writer drones on about how wise this decision is, when suddenly the mindreader's agent with his magic wand appears before the car. "Come," he says, "we are all ready," as if he had not heard, or was incapable of understanding, or refused to believe that the film would not be made. The director stares at him as if hypnotized, stops the car and gets out, the voice of his co-writer becoming more distant and his face no longer visible behind the reflections of sky and trees in the windshield.

The director almost mechanically walks back to the set—suddenly seeming to understand . . . what? that he does not have to understand. He must complete the film that has already been made in his own mind and in our reality because it is beautiful and moving and the actors have reproduced people who have their own life and reality, and they must not be allowed to die. The actors qua characters are brought together behind a curtain drawn by the director, and they march to his direction, now wearing white. They are all pure now (like the girl in white as an inadequate symbol of purity throughout his fantasies) because they have been cleansed of irrelevant "significance" and can now emerge as pure works of art, as abstractions uncontaminated by memory, fantasy, reality, or iconography. The march is led by the director, now holding hands with his own creations, and his final act is to place within the suddenly appearing circus ring the young actor who played his own childhood and the symbol of entertainment and magic—the clown. The fadeout is on his own child-soul piping on a bittersweet lute.

The mindreader's agent was responsible for the decision to complete the film. Why he? Because as the agent of mysterious and magical forces, he epitomizes the role of the artist. It would be absurd for this man to give up his function because he cannot understand its mechanism, just as it would be absurd for the artist not to produce his masterpiece because he cannot understand what its organization or appeal is.

Psychiatrists tease apart threads of human behavior: watch stories of grief, rage, and longing unfold before them; search for the covert behind the manifest; are confronted with paradox; scrutinize and manipulate one relationship as a paradigm of thousands of others; relate in a thousand different ways; are aware of a few and comment upon fewer facets of a whole universe of phenomena; and still insist upon being behavioral scientists. There may come a time when the analysts of behavior who want to break things down into discrete units that can be measured will be able to feed into a computer not only the words transmitted back and forth between therapist and patient, but also the intonations, the gestures, the expressions— the infinite array of metacommunications—and also the memories and associations that each communication and metacommunication brings forth to every level of consciousness in each of the two individuals. The computer may then be able to put all of this data together and come up with something resembling the truth, but of course it won't. Henri Bergson said that science takes a simple gesture and breaks it down into many still photographs, and as science becomes more advanced, the photographs increase in number and sharpness, but it can never capture the essence of the movement. That movement remains something different from the many analyzable photographs of it—interesting as those photographs are in themselves.

The therapist who recognizes love or despair or anger in his patient does not have to analyze bits of data to make that recognition. When we see a friend coming towards us, we don't stop to ask ourselves if the nose, eyes, mouth, or clothing match that of a person we think we know—we either see him as the friend or we don't.

In his ability to resort to intuitive, extrarational and immediate sources of information about his patient without the constant analysis of artificially fragmented bits of data, the psychotherapist is like the artist. But like art, there is good and bad psychotherapy, and one of the best criteria for good art or psychotherapy is the degree of control and consistency pervading the freedom of perception and expression. In art this control may be supplied by aesthetic or iconographic considerations; in psychotherapy it is supplied by conceptual ones.

During a psychotherapeutic session the therapist may view his patient and the relationship between them in psychoanalytic terms, at other times in behaviorist terms or transactional terms; and at still other times, he may abrogate the conceptualization completely and permit himself the necessary luxury of watching the unfolding of a human drama in purely existential terms.

When I was a resident in psychiatry I had a patient who taught me that psychotherapy cannot always be guided by what is known or theorized.

A 25-year-old man entered treatment because he was unable to carry on a conversation with a woman. For two years this symptom had grown progressively more severe and incapacitating. It had begun shortly after the suicide of his young wife after one year of marriage.

He told the story of his marriage during our first interview. He had thought the relationship a happy one. There had been some conflicts with his wife about her previous dependency on her mother in the face of her new alliance with a husband, but all in all they had seemed to be compatible and sensible and capable of confronting and solving problems.

For several weeks prior to her suicide, his wife had been depressed and argumentative. On the day of her death, they arose together as usual and ate breakfast before going to their separate jobs. He usually left first while she had a second cup of coffee. On that morning as he was getting ready to leave, she asked, "Please stay a few minutes to talk with me." He responded, "All right," and sat down, but after another moment she said, "Never mind, you'd better get to work." When he returned that evening, she was dead.

He could not weep. He went through the funeral and the condolences—the whole strained, empty, uncomfortable ritual of family and friends and institutional grief feeling nothing but a numbness inside himself. He mechanically picked up the fabric of his life as a widower at 23. He was not really depressed; he slept and ate well, was not hopeless about the future, anticipated a satisfying career, and saw himself remarrying eventually. He did not look sad. Despite this there was a presence of a peculiar numbness within him at all times—as if all feelings, joy as well as grief, were locked away in some hidden chamber of his soul; and then, there was his symptom, he could not talk to women.

My supervisor and I agreed that this was a pathological grief reaction, that some source of unconscious guilt had interfered with the normal, healthy, painful, necessary process of grieving. My patient had never experienced the weeks of despair, emptiness, yearning, the burning tears that never seem to stop, that wash away the multitude of conflicted feelings that tie human souls together. Our job was to find out why. The patient and I explored his past. He had had good relationships with his parents, friends, and teachers. He was successful and competent at school and work. There had been no previous neurotic symptomatology. One overwhelmingly significant crisis in his life prior to his wife's suicide was the sudden death from heart disease of his mother ten years before. We focused on this event though the early and precipitous loss of his mother seemed to have been adequately grieved and accepted, but certainly it could have left him with a sensitivity to loss that might have fed into his present state. As this focus was sharpened, as we attempted to illuminate the bridge between the deaths ten years apart of the two most important women in his life, something happened. It happened so insidiously that it was several therapy sessions before I realized that it was happening. I found that he was becoming less spontaneous, that his memories and thoughts had become less accessible, and that I was working harder to draw them out. When I stopped drawing him out, I was confronted with a silent patient.

I tested this and said nothing for a total session, and for fifty minutes my patient said nothing. He expressed no curiosity, no dismay, no discomfort, no anger at the silence, nothing.

Armed with my supervisor's experience and advice, I interpreted the patient's silence as a resistance to therapy. We had approached an area in his psychic life that was too laden with anxiety, and his defensive reaction was to be silent. There was no response to the interpretation. When I asked him if he had any thoughts, he said he had not. His mind, he said was a blank, and so I waited.

In years past, during summers, I had swung a pickaxe, waited on tables, and carried garbage pails. In medical school I committed endless pages of information to memory. During my internship I stayed awake more than 40 hours at a time caring for seriously ill patients under impossible circumstances. But never have I found more difficult work than spending 50 minutes with a patient in psychotherapy in total, complete, absolute silence.

He never missed a session and was always on time. I, too, was always there on time, fortified with strong, black coffee to help me stay awake. After several weeks, my supervisor became a little impatient and suggested that perhaps it was time that we tell the patient to start working in therapy or leave. But I decided not to do this. Was it stubbornness in me or was I dimly, subliminally aware of some need on my patient's part for me to wait him out? Seven hours passed in silence. I kept asking myself what use this served. Expensive and urgently needed professional time was being spent. I was learning nothing about my patient, and he was learning nothing about himself. The minutes passed laboriously as if the entire weight of an individual's helplessness and despair hung on the hands of the clock. I became aware of my own impatience. It showed itself to me (and possibly to the patient) as boredom and fatigue. I also began to hypothesize deeper psychopathology in him than I had originally supposed. Was he a severe passive-aggressive personality disorder or even schizophrenic rather than merely neurotic? Then it ended, much more suddenly than it had begun.

During the eighth hour of silence, the patient heard me ask, perhaps with more warmth than he expected, "How are things going?" I said it quietly, just above a whisper. It sounded almost seductive, too seductive, I thought to myself immediately after I uttered it. He looked directly at me as he almost never did. So quickly that I remember marveling at the speed which an emotion can be transformed into a glandular secretion, his eyes became moist. He said, "I've wanted to talk so badly." The words poured out of him. He seemed to be choking his sobs back. He talked of how miserable he was during the long silence, of how he dreaded me, of how he expected me momentarily to throw back my chair in furious disgust and outraged impatience and leave him. Then, within minutes he was remembering the day of his wife's suicide, retelling it as if he were reliving it, staring at the wall opposite as if he were watching it unfold before him. It was practically the same story as told before, but not exactly. He remembered that the night before, they had had an argument, a particularly bitter one. He remembered being annoyed with his wife's grating, conflicted dependency on her mother. He remembered thinking that he himself had lost his mother earlier than he should have and what right did his wife have to complain? His annoyance with her was not quite dissipated by sleep. And now he remembered, and winced with the remembrance, that when his wife asked him to sit and talk with her before going off to work, he had said not "All right" but "Oh, all right" with a sign of impatience, a residue of annoyance, a distinct, unmistakable metamessage of hostility to which his wife could only respond, "No, never mind. You'd better get to work." Then she killed herself.

He wept, sobs racked his body and convulsed his shoulders, and tears flowed down his face. He covered his eyes with his hands, and his fingers were white as they pressed around his eyes. In his broken, miserable and child-sobbing voice, he said, "If only . . . I had been . . . more patient . . . waited for her to talk . . . tell me how bad she felt . . . I could have comforted her . . . and . . . she'd be alive." From that hidden, locked chamber of his soul came an endless wail of guilt-ridden grief, of longing and lost love.

The silence ended, the treatment progressed; and as his grief progressed, he could take a more balanced view of his wife and her death. Eventually he could again express hostility towards her for having done such an incredibly hostile thing towards him; and eventually his grief came to an end and left him free of the painful yearning, guilt, dependency, and helplessness that is the grieving process.[1] He would never forget his wife, but he would not go on missing her so much that his life lost all meaning, hope, and integrity. Within three months his symptoms vanished. He decided to terminate his treatment shortly after becoming engaged to be married.

Later I asked myself how I could have known that the story of the subtle impatience that cut the life thread of his wife could not have been told unless my patience was strong enough to wait for it. He was unconsciously atoning for his own unconscious guilt by placing me in his position. The guilt would have been lessened had I told him to start working or leave, but the therapy would have ended with the agonizing conflict still locked in. It was not scientific fact nor rigid adherence to a process that led me to the result, it was something else, something beyond theory.

The community psychiatrist, no less than the psychotherapist, shares something with the creative artist. The forces of social change and the nature of organizational life are more complex and multifaceted than any theory can encompass. Tolstoy's General Kutozov in *War and Peace* knew about the irrational and inscrutable aspects of war. He was victorious not because he was a brilliant strategist, but because he knew how to abrogate military strategy in the face of the mysterious forces that led a cavalry charge to rally a disintegrated army to victory and that caused the defeat of an overwhelmingly superior force because of a cry of panic.

Social action no less than war requires the ability to abrogate "strategy" as well as to make use of it. Social change is an irrational mixture of rational and extrarational forces. Institutions and individuals both have complex lives, and it is rarely possible to predict with certainty what the ultimate impact on human welfare will be of any institutional change.

Automation, which promised to free mankind from the burden of toil, may bring in its wake undreamed of anguish. Medical science in reducing death rates and lengthening the life expectancy may have condemned mankind to an animal-like struggle for life-space.

A great part of the effort of men to enrich themselves, to increase their freedom and to enhance the quality of their lives has resulted in the reverse. Like Sisyphus, damned to rolling his huge stone up hill, we are engaged in an absurd struggle.

THE PSYCHIATRIST IN SPACE

7

A psychiatrist can accept relatively easily the implications of man's behavior's being influenced by his *social environment*. Community psychiatry is, after all, merely psychodynamic psychiatry with an interchangeable focus on individuals, families, institutions, and communities. A more unsettling revelation awaited me, however: that man's *physical environment* might also have a major impact on his mental health. It appeared that not only the content and substance of man's interpersonal relationships could influence his behavior, but also that their arrangement and structure could be influential.

If, in fact, issues of density and design, of vision, hearing, and distance were salient psychosocial forces, then the community psychiatrist would have to seek alliances not only with acknowledged social change agents, but also with architects, physical facilities planners, demographers, and mortgage bankers.

Let me touch briefly on a few of the discoveries that convinced me that the community psychiatrist must inevitably encompass in his purview the total environment, the interplay of *all* forces, in short, the human ecological system.

The earliest indications that physical density itself seemed to exert an influence on individual behavior derived from the observations of ethologists, the students of animal behavior.

A Swiss animal psychologist named Hediger[1] observed the territorial behavior of wild animals. He described two invisible lines around each animal which determined whether the animal would flee or attack. These lines varied widely from one species to another but were consistent within species. These distances could, however, be modified in captivity. The farther line he called the "flight distance" and the nearer line the "critical distance." When an enemy would approach within the flight distance, our animal would withdraw until that distance had been exceeded. If our animal were cornered or surrounded so that the enemy could come within the critical distance, he would immediately stop withdrawing and begin to stalk the enemy in preparation for attack. In other words, a wild animal's choice of discretion or belligerence is determined by the distance from his enemy.

Lion tamers use this knowledge more than they use whips, guns, and chairs. They place a stool in front of a lion and then approach within his critical distance. The lion begins to stalk the trainer, climbing over the obstacle of the stool, at which point the tamer withdraws beyond the critical distance leaving the animal perched on the stool.

There have been many classic studies on the effects of population density on animal behavior. Among the most famous of these are the observations of Christian[2] on the Sika deer on James Island. Between 1916 and 1955 an original herd of five deer increased to 300 on a half square mile of uninhabited island in Chesapeake Bay. In 1955, Christian examined the organs of five deer that he shot on the island and obtained base line data. Three years later, for no apparent reason, half the deer population died within three months. The next year another large group died until the population of deer stabilized at about 80. Studies of the deer carcasses obtained during this period showed that the cause of death was not starvation nor infection, but the disordered metabolism resulting from hyperfunction of the adrenal glands—the endocrine glands which mediate the organism's response to stress. Animals examined after this period showed smaller adrenal glands, suggesting that the stress that had led to the death of half their population was from the density of the deer.

The most famous studies of the effects of density on animal behavior are those of psychologist John B. Calhoun[3] of the National Institute of Mental Health. Beginning in 1947, Dr. Calhoun placed five pregnant Norway rats in a quarter acre outdoor pen. Even though there was adequate food and an absence of predators, the population stabilized at 150 rats, when within that period of time (28 months) the rats could have produced 50,000 progeny. To discover the reasons why the population stabilized at so low a figure, Calhoun then constructed three 10 ft. by 14 ft. rooms open to observation through the ceiling. Each room was divided into four pens by electrified partitions—each pen having provisions for all the necessities of a rat's existence. Ramps over the partitions connected all but the end two pens.

From his previous observations, Calhoun decided that 48 rats could occupy the room—a colony of 12 rats for each pen if evenly divided. He started with 32 sex-matched rats and kept the ramps in place so that all rats could explore all four pens. His only intervention after that was to remove excess rats over a limit of 80, twice the number that induced discernible stress. He did this to prevent a die-off, as had happened on James Island, so that he might observe successive generations of rats reared in this environment of chronic stress.

Calhoun observed that the two end pens were taken over by a couple of tough, dominant male rats who kept harems of eight to ten females. The remaining 14 male rats distributed themselves in the middle two pens; it was there, when the population began to grow, that Calhoun observed the distortions of behavior that he called the "behavioral sink." He measured the use of food hoppers, and when the hoppers in the middle pens were used three to five times more frequently than those in the end pens, the behavioral sink developed.

There were gross distortions of all aspects of rat behavior. The usually elaborate mating ritual was abandoned, resulting in the rat equivalent of rapine and homosexuality. The usually neat and precise pattern of nest-building was replaced by a sloppy, indifferent process so that the young were often scattered at birth and were frequently eaten.

The social organizational patterns of the Norway rats were disrupted in the "sink" with an unstable and fluid hierarchy's developing out of a previously secure pattern of leadership and followership.

The rats in the end pens did not show any of these abnormal behavior patterns, and, except for a heightened scrutiny and protectiveness of their turfs, they were entirely normal.

Dr. Calhoun's experiments and observations were much more detailed and subtle than can be quickly summarized here, but I want to stop here because I suspect that most readers will have already made up their minds by this point that crowding causes disturbed behavior in humans too. Though this is probably true, there is no hard evidence that contemporary urban problems are the result of overcrowding.

Overpopulation may yet prove to be the gravest threat mankind has ever or ever will face. The image of starving, unsheltered millions in India is a terrifying one. That our own population growth is rapidly approaching a date when it will become irreversible is just as terrifying. According to the demographer Philip Hauser,[4] even with a generous 50 per cent reduction in our birth rate, there would still be an absolute increase of five to six million people each year in this country. A conservative estimate is that by the year 2000, there will be a hundred million more people added to the cities of the United States. That is half the current total population of the entire country. Migration patterns are such that as the population grows, there will be an increasingly rapid migration from rural to urban areas as I have touched on in a previous chapter.

Increasingly dense megalopoli will grow in the Northeast Corridor, around the Gulf of Mexico, and from San Francisco to San Diego. Barring the development of new metropolitan areas in the plains, our rural areas will become even more sparsely populated. While it will take another third of a century for a hundred million people to be added to our numbers, only fifteen years thereafter will see still another hundred million people added to engorge the cities. In roughly 50 years from now, our population will double.

Small comfort it is that a massive national effort of birth control or population dispersal might maintain our own population growth within manageable limitations. Even if we do not assume a human responsibility to help feed the rest of mankind, can we really expect that the technologically advanced, controlled and well-fed nations of the world will be secure when surrounded by millions upon millions of hungry and desperate people?

This grim picture is of the future. Let us resist the temptation to become nihilistic and hopeless before it is absolutely necessary. Let us not distort the facts by assuming that all contemporary problems are due to overcrowding.

A Frenchman, Paul Chombard de Lauwe,[5] found that the number of residents per dwelling unit was not related to social or physical pathology but that the number of square meters per person per dwelling unit was relevant. When the space available was *less* than eight to ten square meters per person per unit, pathology doubled. From this he concluded that illness and crime were linked with spatial crowding. Unfortunately, he did not correct for social class and other issues which may be concomitants of overcrowding, and which may be more salient pathogenic forces.

He could not, furthermore, adequately explain why there was also an increase in pathology when the available space rose *above* 14 square meters per person per unit.

Another bit of information that should warn us against jumping to the conclusion that urban problems are mainly the result of heightened density comes from the city of Hong Kong. This is the densest spot in the entire world and yet it has a relatively low rate of social pathology.

The justification for laying the problems of inner-city life in this country at the doorstep of overcrowding is inadequate. Before we consider overcrowding as the basis of riots, crime, mental illness, and high infant death rates, we should pay attention to unemployment, segregation, inadequate health facilities, powerlessness, hopelessness, and alienation, as these may be more meaningfully and immediately related to pathology than density is.

We frequently hear statements to the effect that programs of social improvement will never be effective until birth control can be imposed upon the urban poor. I find it curious that the people who insist on this have rarely been ardent exponents of programs of social improvement. I am thus a little suspicious of people who refer with too much emphasis to the birth rate of the poor. It sounds a little too much like an abrogation of responsibility and an almost self-righteous assignation of blame. Family planning information and techniques should be very available to the inner-city poor, just as they are to everyone else, because only through birth control measures can any person have a sense of mastery and control over his own and his family's destiny. To imply that the inner-city Negro should have a maximum family size imposed upon him, however, and not impose the same limitations on the middle-class suburbanite is to be arrogant, inhumane, and unscientific.

Whether or not density is a salient influence on human behavior, other fascinating studies demonstrate the effects of other environmental forces relating to space.

Urban anthropologist Edward T. Hall has developed an intriguing field of study known as proxemics.[6] Proxemics deals with the varying kinds of behavior human beings exhibit depending upon their distance from one another. According to Hall there are invisible lines around us that distinguish between intimate, personal, social, and public kinds of behavior. Hall found that these distances were remarkably constant within cultures but varied widely from one culture to another.

In the United States, the intimate distance extends up to 18 inches. This is the zone of love-making or fighting. There is physical contact and eye to eye contact. Vocalization, if any, tends to be at the level of a whisper.

Personal distance extends from 18 inches to four feet. This is the zone of conversation, close friendship, and psychotherapy. The voice level is moderate, and the unique individuality of each person within this space is acknowledged. Touching may or may not take place depending on the situation, but it is usually permissible. An uninvited invasion of this space is an offensive intrusion.

Social distance extends from four feet to twelve feet in this country. This is the area of impersonal business and casual social gathering. Office furniture is designed to keep people in that space: the more important the official, the more distant is his position at his desk from that of his subordinate. Professors of psychiatry frequently have two arrangements in their offices. One is at a spacious desk around which residents and students are kept at a comfortably subordinate distance; and another arrangement at a coffee table around which a few comfortable chairs are positioned so the professor can talk with patients or peers within a personal zone.

Public distance is measured at twelve feet and beyond. This is outside the circle of personal involvement. The voice is louder and speech tends to be more formal, planned, and impersonal.

A little imagination or observation demonstrates how much our behavior is dictated by these distances.

I recall riding the New York subway system regularly during rush hours when people were squeezed together as tightly as they could possibly be. Under other circumstances and with a trifle more choice of partners, the intimacy might have been enjoyable. In the subway, with occasional exceptions, the experience is unpleasant and every attempt is made to deny the invasion of intimate distance. People may be literally on top of one another in the subway, but they never acknowledge each other's presence—any eye to eye contact would be such an acknowledgment, thus is it strictly, if tacitly, forbidden. God help the man who should look at the woman he is touching during the rush hour!

These distances or zones, these bubbles of varying behavior around us, are actually extensions of our personalities. Our spatial requirements do not end with our skins.

Dr. Hall discovered that Arabs have much closer zones than Westerners have. An Arab feels the need to smell an interlocutor, thus in a social encounter the Arab might approach within a Westerner's personal or intimate zones.

The Westerner feels uncomfortable and moves away to what to him is a more appropriate social distance. The Arab, unconsciously, approaches to avoid what would be for him a more public distance. The result may be an unintended, in fact, unconscious offense. Obviously, diplomats need to be taught about proxemics to avoid even more international incidents than we already have.

That issues such as these have direct clinical significance was demonstrated by psychiatrist Humphry Osmond.[7] From his observations, such as comparing the kinds of interactions which occur in railway waiting rooms in which people tend to keep apart and in sidewalk cafes in which people tend to get together, he developed a theory of spaces. Sociofugal spaces, like the waiting room, tend to keep people apart; sociopetal spaces, like the sidewalk cafe, tend to bring them together.

Dr. Osmond and psychologist Robert Sommer[8] studied the clean, modern geriatric ward in their hospital and noticed that the longer the patients stayed on the ward, the less they seemed to talk to one another. The patients seemed to become even less animated, alive, motivated, and hopeful after a while than they were when first admitted. On the assumption that the sociofugal structure of the ward had something to do with this, they experimented with various kinds of cafeteria seating arrangements and discovered that corner situations with people at right angles to each other produced six times as many conversations as face to face situations across a 36 inch table and twice as many as a side by side arrangement. Using such information and taking into consideration such issues as the patients' proprietary interests in "their" furniture and the resistance of the staff to ward changes,[9] the investigators redesigned the interior of the ward to a much more sociopetal and hence therapeutic environment.

An extraordinary social scientist, city planner, and inventor, Mayer Spivack,[10] has studied the anti-therapeutic monstrosities that some architects have imposed upon mental patients. In spanking-new, modern mental hospitals, Spivack has discovered hallways designed in such a configuration that a distant figure appears to be suspended in space with his head unattached to his body because of the light sources. In other areas, the lighting is such that an approaching person cannot be recognized until he is well within the personal zone of space, a situation which may be highly threatening to the vulnerable life-space of a schizophrenic. Other environmental factors studied by Spivack were rooms the scale of which produced upsetting illusions—both of the room size and scale and of the occupants—and interior glass walls which created illusions of the person approaching the glass walk through solid walls behind the glass. One of his most incredible examples of a bad environment for peace of mind was a promenade for patients that was so long and unvarying in its design that the person lost all reckoning of time-distance factors. Even at a rapid pace a normal person felt that he was on a treadmill. One can imagine the message that such a promenade would give to the emotionally disabled individual slowly trudging along. He would at least wonder, "Can I ever reach my destination?" and on reflection would not be able to distinguish where he had been.

Aspects of the physical design of mental hospitals or community mental health centers are not aesthetic niceties imposed upon their more significant programmatic aspects.

Their structural design is as fundamental to the impact of the mental health services program on patients as anything that will take place within their walls. The behavior of patients on the back wards of state hospitals was programmed by the impersonal, inhumane, undignified design of wards and day rooms. The rows of identical beds, the absence of private storage spaces, the locked windows behind detention screens, the "easy-to-clean" floors, the lines of benches before the untouchable television set, the "shatter-proof" cups, and the always-visible-to-the-public toilets that flush automatically signalled the patients how to behave. The environment said to the patient, "You will be an undistinguished, irresponsible, helpless, unclean, destructive, uncommunicative, incontinent animal." The patients, their egos already shattered by all the genetic, biochemical, developmental, and environmental demons of mental illness, obliged.

A recent publication[11] describes the process and results of truly collaborative efforts by psychiatrists and architects to design six comprehensive community mental health centers. The models, themselves, are not so significant as the demonstrations of creative dialogues between the professions—dialogues geared to a marriage of form and function in the interest of mental health. The two professions were joined as one: specialists in therapeutic environment.

Psychiatrists can really have little argument about the need to become actively involved in the design of mental hospitals and community mental health centers. If this is so, then all that I have been saying about the psychiatrist's involvement in the total community similarly demands his involvement with the physical design of the community and its institutions. The community psychiatrist is, after all, concerned with the creation and development of competent institutions the functions of which enhance the mental health of the residents. The activities of schools, police stations, libraries, playgrounds, taverns, and similar community agents have the potential for enriching life and preventing mental illness as well as providing for narrowly defined social needs. The physical design of such institutions—as well as their service programs—can be part of the community psychiatrist's challenge. This becomes evident to any behavioral scientist fortunate enough to participate in the planning of a new institution, a new service, or a new town.

For a nation going through an acute failure of nerve about its urban condition, the new town idea offers a small but brilliant light of hope. It is a revival of utopianism cleansed of the precious, naive, totalitarian colorings to which it was previously subjected. It is a revival of utopianism in a time of futility, desperation, panic, and scapegoating. It is the emergence of a beautiful idea at a time when beautiful ideas seem no longer to exist. The idea is to bring together men of goodwill and sophistication, of imagination and experience, and let them plan a city for people!

Ideas come with their parasites just as organisms do. A great many things have been passed off as new towns when they were a rehash of middle-class, suburban developments thrown around a shopping center, or an outrageously expensive single-family dwelling unit institution for the aged, or a company town. A new town worthy of the name should contain a healthy slice of all social classes. It should have its own economic base and not be dependent upon a single industry. It should have its own cultural, educational, social and health institutions and not depend upon an adjacent metropolis. In short, it should be a city capable of providing for a rich and full life for all of its residents even if it were dropped in the middle of a desert. What an opportunity for a community psychiatrist! He can meet with the economists, city planners, architects, traffic engineers, educators, lawyers, social scientists, and if he can learn to talk with them and they with him, a new human biotype may emerge in which *individuals and institutions can be responsive to one another.*

A profound skepticism is generally the first response to discussions of planned communities. As a first response, it is the only intelligent one. Humanistic and nonauthoritarian sensibilities can only be offended by an introduction to the idea of a city whose residents are provided for before they exist. It takes repeated exposure of the idea before you can be comfortable with it. At that point you realize that the alternative to planning is not freedom or spontaneity, but arbitrary and poor planning. Rather than springing from the interplay of vested interests and considerations of realpolitik, the life of a community can be generated out of a rational and humane concern for all the residents.

Our free and spontaneous "unplanned cities" have resulted in air that stings the eyes and irritates the lungs, water fouled by sewage and detergents, housing that shelters as many rats as people, and an economic condition that irrevocably separates the "haves" from the "have-nots." "Freedom and spontaneity" have created the conditions of violent, outraged, impatient, and reckless frustration not only expressed in rioting, but also in the response to rioting. It has produced not a body of unemployed men, but a body of unemployable men—a caste of hereditary poverty. It has produced a situation in which hardware technology has so far outstripped our knowledge of its implications that while some are still shouting that welfare recipients ought to be "kicked off their doles" and into work, others will be convinced of the economic necessity of producing an entire nation of consumers to keep the automated factories functioning. It has produced a period in our history in which we fight an incredible and extremely costly war while facing the imminent death by starvation of millions on that same continent. It has resulted in a time that future historians may point to as the death of American civilization.

New towns are not, of course, city states, and the latitude for planning is not as great as some might desire. County, state, and federal constraints continue to exist, as do the economic realities of American capitalism. Within these constraints, however, there exists the ability to create new institutions and redefine old ones in such a way that as many people as possible can have as wide as possible a degree of choice in how to live their lives.

Libraries might have terraces where people can drink beer and converse about books instead of dehumanized stacks in which people are shushed. Rather than being cloistered in museums, works of art might be displayed in parks and on street corners so that a Picasso painting can be looked at while one waits for a bus or has a picnic. Supermarkets might have nurseries to look after the children while their mothers shop. Perhaps people can row to a shopping center rather than drive. Religious groups might be able to share facilities and functions and begin a local ecumenical movement. Theaters might be designed for actors rather than for spectators and the entire community might have the option of participating in drama—not geared to the end of a public performance, but as an end in itself. Schools might be located in factories and factories located in parks so the lines between education, work, and recreation become indistinct and eventually disappear. This would be a reintegration of life rather than a fragmentation by arbitrary clock-oriented assignments. Adolescents may be given a responsible and formal stake in society by having their own institutions such as hotels, carnivals, and police activities. Law enforcement and correctional institutions may themselves be redefined as preventive and rehabilitative forces, with policemen functioning not as an army of occupation but as community organizers, group recreation workers, and counselors, armed with knowledge, understanding, physical prowess and self-control rather than with guns.[12]

When asked what kinds of social problems might be expected in the new town of Columbia, Maryland, its developer, James Rouse, responded with a weary patience, "New ones." The planners of new cities can never be so naive as to assume that social problems can be planned out of existence. But what they can do, and what has never been done before, is plan in such a way that mistakes can be undone. The institutions in new towns should be more like circus tents than monuments. They should be planned in a flexible and pluralistic way with a sense of lightheartedness rather than solemnity. It is the death of imagination to take itself too seriously.

The city should be beautiful beyond words, constructed with grace and humor, and, I suppose if my ideas were carried to their absurd extreme, it would be built out of such materials as ice or paper so that it could be melted down or thrown away and redone each week.

The major reason the social planning for new towns has to be done with a sense of limited liability and impermanence is that the guiding principle for any wholesome environment must be self-determination; and once the residents exist, they may have different ideas and inclinations. As with any individual, group, or social system, a greater amount of structure, guidance, and support is necessary at first than later. Once the city has an identity and a body politic, the behavioral scientists and mental health custodians and ideologues will have to permit the city to determine its own destiny. It may choose to continue an alliance with the planners, to use them as consultants or facilitators, but this must remain a choice of the residents. If they choose to turn the city into a microcosm of the worst of urban America, that, too, must be their choice. There are too many other heralds of the death of democracy for the new town movement to assist in the burial.

Apart from the timing and phasing of planning activities, there is a spatial constraint on what the planners can manipulate. The individual, his family, and his home are inviolate. As activities involve increasingly larger groups and more public spaces, they become fairer game for the planners.

A community not only must have rules and sanctions, but also must have an attitude toward these rules. The brilliant sociologist Erving Goffman, in a study of total institutions,[13] talks about the two kinds of adjustments that patients make in mental hospitals. The primary adjustment is that which results in a strict adherence to rules and regulations, a "fitting in" to the organization's often arbitrarily decided standards. Because the regulations in hospitals are frequently for the convenience of the institution rather than for the needs of the patient, a primary adjustment is not always the most therapeutic one. The secondary adjustment is that made by the patient who finds ways of operating between or in violation of the regulations of the institution so as to assert his own individuality or satisfy his wants. While this may be annoying to the administrators of the hospital, it is not infrequently in the best interests of the patient.

Whether in a family or in an institution or a community, individuals cannot be placed in the bind of being told both to obey and to disobey rules. It is not possible to encourage systematically a secondary adjustment. It is possible, however, to *tolerate* the secondary adjustment as long as it is not destructive.

In one planned community, some very handsome sculpture and fountains were designed specifically so that children could climb over and through them. The residents were told that this was permitted. Perhaps as the result of a combination of this official permissiveness and the kinds of families that were attracted to such an environment (liberal, middle-class parents who have difficulty setting limits for their children), the preadolescents in the community engaged in such acts as putting detergents in the fountains and defacing the sculpture. They seemed to be pushing the limits of permissiveness. One wonders if this would have been avoided had the community, rather than encouraging climbing on the sculpture, just not become very exercised when it was done. Climbing rather than the more destructive behavior would then have been the deviant act—the secondary adjustment.

For years in New York City this philosophy of tolerance has been practiced by the Police and Fire Departments with reference to the turning on of fire hydrants by the children of Harlem so they could splash in the water. The hydrants were shut off by the police with the benign, unfrustrated, and sensible knowledge that as soon as they left, the hydrants would be turned back on again. It was a perfectly functional secondary adjustment by the kids and a consistent, functional, and tolerant response by the police. *Restrictions can be established with the expectation of their being marginally exceeded.*

Insight into behavioral responses and a different perspective on social policies are among the kinds of contributions the community psychiatrist can make to the planning efforts of new towns. Actually doing so entails his seeking out liaisons with political and financial forces that he is rarely accustomed to facing. It also entails his becoming as sophisticated about the nature of organizations as he is about individuals.

But organizations can be sick too.

THE MENTAL HEALTH OF ORGANIZATIONS

8

Community psychiatry is the realm of invisible extensions of people beyond their skins. Man's behavior is influenced by his physical environment; his identity by his family; his self-esteem by his car; his aspirations by his peers. We live as much outside our physical selves as within, and rather than saying that a man's soul inhabits his body, it would be more accurate to say that it surrounds it like the atmosphere surrounds the earth.

There are crystallizations of this atmosphere of "self-ness" in other people and in institutions. I cannot conceive of myself except in the context of people I love and need and of organizations whose goals I have decided to adopt or change.

So much of what we "are" is determined by the nature of our organizations that it would be as useful to talk about their health and illness, their competence and durability, as our own.

Marc Fried[1] has described a theory of "complementarity" between the ego and a social system. A weak and disordered ego may be complemented by a strong and well organized milieu without a breakdown. On the other hand, according to Fried, a highly integrated and secure ego can endure in the face of a weak and fragile social system in which less competent egos would decompensate.

Fried's theory is an attractive and neat theory, but I suspect that the relationship of mental health to organizational life is more complicated than this. It may be a matter of the number of social systems around each of us, or their pertinence or their values as well as their stability. We may even find that, to speak the language of mental health, some organizations may have to be deliberately unstable or ephemeral.

There are two hazards connected with the inclination of individuals to extend their egos into organizations and institutions. The first is that many organizations are not run in such a way as to recognize that the welfare of individuals is at stake. The second hazard is the tendency of individuals to feel that any organization they have joined must close its doors immediately after them. We want to feel that our groups are exclusive and sharply defined. We must know where our family, race, and nation begin and end so that we can feel intact and uncontaminated. In our constant search for alliances and delineated communities, we are at the same time defining aliens and enemies.

Let me begin with the first hazard of this joining instinct, that the organization we invest ourselves in may be insensitive to us as individuals.

The most significant social system in our lives is that in which housekeeping, child-rearing, and sexual functions are performed, the family. In our society, the decision to marry and have children is the most important one a person can make. More of what he is and will be is determined by that decision than by any other. A greater investment of self is required in marriage than in any other contractual arrangement in life. Ideally, the marriage partner no longer imagines himself the center of the universe, and he finds himself needing to be concerned about the security and satisfaction of someone else, as much as he is about his own. This entails responsibility, restrictions, and restraints. If we were to look at marriage dispassionately and objectively, we would ask ourselves why we should marry.

There are times and situations in which the asking of an unanswerable question is itself symptomatic of a severe conflict. A little girl does not ask why it is better to be a girl than a boy unless she is doubtful about herself and is already convinced that it is not better to be a girl. It is only because she is insecure about her identity that she asks the question. A schizophrenic will ask why he should bother with sexual intercourse when masturbation is more satisfying to him. There are no answers to these questions except to state the obvious, that many little girls are perfectly happy staying little girls and that most adults seem to find more satisfaction in sexual intercourse than masturbation.

In the same way, there is no answer to or argument

with the question, "Why should I marry and have children?" With rare exceptions (the hippie culture which is too new to evaluate and the Israeli kibbutz which is only a slight modification of family life), the prevailing Western civilized form of combining sex, homemaking, and companionship is marriage. Yet, when this "ideal" primary organization, the family, is exclusive, it can be terribly destructive. The family is a remarkable invention of our species; it occupies a hallowed and preeminent place in our lives. Because of this, the individual, child, or adult who is excluded from it, whose welfare is sacrificed by it, carries a sorrowful burden. We know all too well that families find ways of isolating, ignoring, or scapegoating one or another of its members (as in the family I described in Chapter 1). There are unspoken and unrecognized compacts, myths, silences (some quiet, others screaming) that permit families to identify a member as "the troubled one" to allay anxiety in the other members.

Let me go on to another level of organizational and institutional life, one in which discussion of individual welfare until very recently seemed irrelevant. I refer to the institution known as "work."

Not so long ago, the most civilized nations of the world did not even consider the possibility of deference to the rights of the working man. I suppose, considering the history of human affairs, we should be grateful for small favors. Early capitalism in the throes of the Industrial Revolution was filled with horrors: windowless factories, 14-hour work days, brutal supervision. People were exploited, exhausted, and discarded as self-replenishing, endlessly available supplies of beasts of burden. Children had their youth, beauty, energy, and hope wrung from them by machines of industry, and the children were transformed into some kind of horrible, fertile senescence. Labor was a commodity, a faceless, mindless, soulless ingredient in the production of wealth for a privileged few.

The Protestant Ethic that gave capitalism its early nurturing was raped by its own offspring as the drive to profit and power resulted in having men and women and small children treated as means rather than ends in themselves.

Somehow things changed. The apocalyptic threats of Marxism, the intrepid and tireless union organizers, and perhaps, perhaps the glimmerings of conscience in the sons of the empire builders resulted in a less murderous form of capitalism. The horrors of the industrial revolution with its love of machines was replaced with the rumblings of the social revolution.

Now, even the nation that was conceived in a Marxist revolution has become fully bureaucratized. And the most conservative, capitalistic, and affluent country in the world actually talks about the elimination of poverty, and its labor unions have become smug and swollen with affluence. One might even be tempted to say that except for the hard-core poor, American capitalism has done pretty well by any standard of decency and practicality.

But the hard-core poor, the unemployed and unemployable urban Negro, the rural white in Appalachia, the Spanish-American migrant laborer, and the dispossessed Indian are rather difficult exceptions to make. There are too many of them and their conditions too deplorable for us to be comfortable about American society. But even putting them aside for a moment, one has to ask what other human values have been forgotten by progressive capitalism.

An official of a major union predicted to me recently that during the final third of this century, organized labor, collective bargaining, and strikes will be focused not on wages nor fringe benefits, but on something called "human dignity." This will have profound implications to organizational life in this country. It means that the working man will not be content with a measure of safety, security, and affluence from his job and that his demands will be for a whole new dimension of satisfactions—demands that his integrity and worth as an individual be guaranteed by his employer.

Having barely shaken off an authoritarian, exploitative, dehumanized image of employee relations, this may come as a bit of a shock. We have just begun to accept the idea that an organization may not arbitrarily threaten the financial security and bodily safety of an employee and now organizations will be told that they must assume responsibility for the mental health, emotional satisfaction, and sense of identity of a worker.

One can already hear the anguished cries of outrage from industrialists, merchants, administrators, and, most of all, government officials. "We have work to do. We must produce and distribute goods and services. We have a mission, a sensitive responsibility, a sacred trust, we cannot turn ourselves into an autistic social agency catering to the endless demands of our own employees."

There will be some insincerity in this outrage because the managers of many enterprises have already become concerned about the satisfaction and self-esteem of one element in the organizations: the managers themselves.

Executives of every conceivable kind of organization have been going through a hypomanic dance of leadership training, sensitivity training, T-groups, managerial grids, et cetera.[2] The practitioners and salesmen of these practices deny that they are doing psychotherapy, but they claim to modify behavior through group process. They deny that there are psychological and social hazards to their practices, yet they frequently keep a psychiatrist available to pick up the pieces of individuals "who had previous emotional problems anyway." They espouse a philosophy of permissiveness and pluralism and yet see themselves as changing the practices and policies of huge organizations. They insist on the voluntariness of the process, but do not seem to be aware of the informal and subtle constraints upon subordinates to participate against their wishes when the president of a company signs a contract for such training. The most glaring contradiction is that while they espouse a nonhierarchical and antibureaucratic ideology, their activities have centered almost exclusively on top and middle management.

Management has embraced these techniques with abandon. Executive training programs have adopted a rhetoric of mental health and social science. *Fortune Magazine* and the *Harvard Business Review* read like journals of existentialism and social psychology. Now we hear executives discussing theories of ethical behavior.[3] Instead of the old image of the captain of industry bellowing his orders to a trembling crew, piloting his enterprise by brute strength and visceral wisdom, leaving in his wake a ruination of natural and human resources, we have a new corporate image: the professional manager, part psychologist, part systems analyst, part social philosopher. We see corporation presidents devoting themselves to the elimination of poverty, segregation, and urban blight, espousing with sincerity and warmth and wisdom an ideology of social justice, equal opportunity, and full employment.

The old manager was interested in wealth and power. The new one is concerned also with his image and his self-esteem. The old manager was uncultured, boorish, unlovely. The new image is of a manager, youthful, healthy, lithe; a magnificent merger of affluence, grace, and a social conscience. It is an image that would make the robber barons puke. It should make us all puke.

The sham is that the executive adorns himself with the rhetoric of social justice and egalitarianism, and so enchanting is the image that he believes in it.[4] The sensitivity trainees and the T-groupers and the managerial gridders believe it too. They see the new corporate image as a reincarnation of humanistic democracy. The whole scene is like some kind of narcissistic orgy in the Executive Washroom. It is as relevant to the blue collar worker as a trip to the moon is to an Indian peasant.

The "human resources" school of management with its nonhierarchical egalitarian, pluralistic, collaborative, libertarian ideas seems to carry the full weight of every sacred tenet of participatory democracy. It turned away from the intellectual dishonesty of the old "human relations" school that grew out of the Mayo studies at Hawthorne and that were interpreted to mean that the appearance of responsiveness on the part of supervisors would maintain morale in subordinates regardless of the response.[5] It certainly promised a breath of fresh air after the rigid, unfeeling, authoritarian trappings of traditional organizational life, but in practice, it is the people who need it least that benefit from such progressive ideas of administration. It is middle and top management that is encouraged to become informal and free, to develop task forces for problem solving rather than bureaucracies. As always, it is the man on the bottom, the man most in need of money, self-esteem, a sense of participation, job security, and organizational identity who gets least of everything. His prospects of helping to shape the destiny of an organization, of having a sense of control and mastery within a social system are quite few even in those companies that pay the greatest heed to "human resources" theories of administration. It is a credentialed kind of democracy that rides to the conference rooms treating the elevator operator as if he were a part of the machine. It steps aside and lowers its voice, perhaps a little self-consciously, as it passes the janitor-mop part of the organization. Its rhetoric and beauty are transmitted through clerk-typists who might as well be as electrically motivated as their machines.

Either work should provide the opportunity for creative imagination and a sense of dignity or it should not. If it should then all human labor should provide that opportunity. If some jobs cannot be freed from drudgery or monotony or are so opprobrious that a man cannot take any joy in the labor of it, then it should be performed only intermittently or with other compensations.

What would happen if we were to say to the employees of an organization, "Our job is to produce transistor radios (or distribute merchandise or administer a grant-in-aid program). You will all be paid an adequate salary. You may work as little or as much as you like. You may try your skills at any level of the organization and at any task for as long a period as you like. If you wish guidance or training at any or all skills, this will be provided; otherwise there will be no supervision. The spiritual or financial profits of the enterprise will be shared equally." Almost everyone tends to anticipate a period of testing out, disorganization, and unproductiveness in such a situation. The interpretation of what would ultimately happen is not based on empirical evidence, because there is none. Either you believe man is inclined to want to work, to participate in a communal effort, and take pride in the results, in which case you see some hope in such an enterprise, or you believe that man is lazy, self-indulgent, unresourceful, and individualistic, in which case only chaos and atrophy are seen as the result. The other alternative, of course, is that some men will fall into one group and others into the other, but presumably such an enterprise could accommodate both groups.

But let us assume once again, that there is no such thing as a fixed human nature. Let us for a moment believe that man is a highly pluralistic and adaptable phenomenon. If this is so, what we would be doing in the creation of such an organization is creating the possibility for new kinds of human behavior. Creating an institution that permits, encourages, or rewards egalitarian, nonhierarchical, noncompetitive and communal efforts may then be tantamount to redefining the nature of man. More correctly, it would permit other aspects and potentials of man to become visible and preeminent, different from those that have been exploited in the past.

The stylish thing now is to imply or promise that organizations recreated in a more humanistic, democratic, and nonbureaucratic mold will become more productive or profitable. It would be nice if this were true, and maybe it is, but to sell humanism and compassion on the market place is to perpetuate a view of mankind that forever pre-cludes humanism and compassion. It reminds me a bit of the short story by James Joyce called "The Retreat."

The story is about a group of businessmen in Dublin who decide that they need some kind of spiritual re-awakening, a moral douche to cleanse themselves of a mer-cenary, middle-class, mercantile state of mind. They go on a Catholic retreat looking forward to a combination of pastoral innocence and liturgical captivity. As they ap-proach the experience, there is within them a state of mutual agitation, a trembling anticipation of a profound, moving, life-shaking experience. What they are finally confronted with is not the impassioned, soul-gripping voice of a minister of the Lord holding out a vision of joyous and loving union with God, not a conversion experience, not a beatification, but a business deal. To reach his would-be penitents, the practical-minded priest offered a huckster's pitch of Heaven, a graceless, joyless, soulless Pascal's bet—a bargain of an eternity with Christ. It was as if the businessmen and the Church had gone to visit each other at the same time, each arriving at the other's home and finding it empty and locked against them.

The soft-hearted and hard-headed social psychologists who see themselves as the cutting edge of a sensitive and sophisticated social revolution may be putting themselves into a similar bind by insisting that humane organizations are "good business." I would be inclined to allow more room for the extrarational forces in society. At a time when the affluent and powerful are looking uncomfortably and restlessly at the clenching of fists around them, when even the Mafia is searching for legitimacy and respect, we should continue to appeal to what might, in fact, have always been there, a sense of justice and compassion.

We should be talking about the creation and re-creation of organizations with missions and motives oriented towards the well-being of the people within them. Instead of promising greater profits or productivity and appealing to a market place mentality, we might assure a functional viability, an adequacy of output, and a moral purpose.

If we are going to be concerned about mental health, one thing we should not promise is organizational immortality. This has to do with the second hazard connected with our penchant for identifying with organizations. Not only are organizations frequently insensitive to us, but they may amplify some of our less wholesome instincts.

We seem to invest our organizations with the same need for immortality, immutability, and predominance as ourselves. "Our church," "our club," "our office," "our nation" must endure and prevail. What a wealth of exploitation lies in that tendency to expand our own narcissism into organizations. The "I'd rather fight than switch" or "better dead than red" instinct has brought wealth and power to those who could appeal to it and untold misery to mankind.

There may have been a time in the development of man when tribal loyalty played some species-preserving function. But like many others, this instinct has the capacity to run wild. Having become more or less convinced that personal immortality is not within our grasp, we have turned with a desperate hunger to groups and institutions to carry the dusty imprints of our lives. We find ourselves fighting for these groups with the same ferocity that we fight for ourselves.

Group identification and loyalty have aspects that are supportive of mental health, but when carried to the extreme of chauvinism, bigotry, and war, a whole new dimension of destructive forces takes over. There is no inevitable reason why group identification must be carried to the degree of exclusiveness and intensity that nationalistic wars, religious crusades, and racial prejudices suggest. It is possible for investment of one's self in groups to be of limited liability: a short-term, functional, pragmatic and flexible investment. At various times and for various purposes, one may consider one's self a Harlemite or a Negro or a Republican or a New Yorker or an American or a member of the human race. It would be consistent with mental health to have the widest option of *in*clusiveness in various groups.

Occasionally individuals have manifested this ability, and mankind has always been enriched by them. Erik Erikson described Gandhi's inclusive sense of identity.[6] Even at the height of his struggle for Indian independence, Gandhi never saw the British as an enemy to be beaten or destroyed. His investment in groups was sufficiently fluid and inclusive to make him see himself as a brother even to his adversaries. This explains how he could be a victorious leader without being a warrior. He could not hate, and he could not kill because it would be part of himself that he would be destroying.

We have tended to create organizations of government, of production, of social welfare, and even of recreation that forge identities of exclusiveness rather than inclusiveness. This has generated a mad, uncontrolled instinct for nationalism, partisanship, and adversity that colors every aspect of our lives. We feel we have to choose sides and make war, even if sides do not exist and have no need to exist. The final comment on the absurdity of war was Swift's in *Gulliver's Travels*. The Big-endians and the Little-endians of Lilliput were carrying on a fight to the finish about which end of the egg was to be cracked open each morning. The great struggle on the planet Earth in the middle of the 20th Century has only added a few conceptual refinements to the wars of Lilliput.

We have to learn how to create ephemeral institutions just as we have learned to accept mortality. We have to learn how to let go, how to let something die. Once we have done that, we can then have organizations that exist for the performance of tasks rather than the artificial creation of tasks to maintain the existence of the organizations. The pseudo-morphs of democracy, the arteriosclerotic bureaucracies, the sphinctered, faceless forms of management, the not quite living but deathless hives of meaningless, empty, dehumanized activity, the Eichmann nests —all this can be replaced by a view of society that permits an organization to die when it is no longer viable. To die, or to be rejuvenated.[7] We have kept our decrepit but undying institutions away from the youths who might have breathed new life into them. We have waited for youth to turn into the withered, enfeebled, inflexible, self-indulgent, hopelessness we call "maturity" before we have let them be trusted with the precious keys to society.

When we have become less frightened of change, which is the challenge of youth, we will find it less necessary to kill. God help us for all those we have killed because of our fear of change!

THE PHYSICIAN AND SOCIAL CHANGE

9

The doctor who extends his skills and efforts from his individual patients to the community and thus becomes a public health agent has not lost his identity as a physician. Nor has the doctor who goes further and becomes involved with political and economic and social forces that have an impact on health lost his identity as a physician.

What determines that identity as a physician? Certainly not technique, for what lies in common between psychotherapy and neurosurgery? I feel that the persona of a physician is made up a certain kind of conscience, a clinical conscience. It is a sense of responsiveness and responsibility in the face of pain and helplessness. It comes from the revelation that despite his inadequacy and ignorance, people place their lives in the hands of the physician and entrust to him their bodies and minds. I write of the idea of the physician. Of course, not all doctors carry this clinician's conscience. I do not know if most physicians do. I do not even know if the most able of them do. But the idea of responsibility and commitment adheres to the idea of the physician more unalterably than any other aspect of the physician's identity.

The psychiatrist who widens his perspective to include mental health as well as mental illness, prevention as well as treatment, social systems and organizations as well as individuals; the psychiatrist who becomes in effect a student and intervenor in the field of human ecology is, nonetheless, a psychiatrist. His ultimate motivation lies in the well-being, the happiness, the freedom, or the mental health of individuals, but more of them than can be treated as his own patients.

The community psychiatrist is more a clinician than a researcher, for it is the clinician's sensitivity to suffering that unsuits him to the methodical and contemplative life of the researcher. The frontiers of the known, the truth, the laws of behavior have less meaning to the clinician than cries of distress. For this reason, it is crucial that the community psychiatrist never lose his base in clinical psychiatry. The ability to evaluate the depth and dynamics of a patient's distress is the guiding principle of his professionalism. Some regular part of his time should be allotted to clinical work.

The abiding reason for having the community psychiatrist continue to treat patients is his occasionally having an experience that will remind him with raw intensity that his position is absurd. There cannot be a harmonious, consistent, pure, and satisfying system of thought and action in this game. It is full of necessary contradictions.

After expressing and implementing a belief that mental illness and mental health do not entirely reside within the individual, after abrogating an authoritarian model of medical care, after criticizing society's standards of normalcy, I found myself one day evaluating an acutely psychotic patient. His ties with reality were pulling apart like cotton batting. His thoughts dissipated before they could be uttered. He alternated between tears, exhilaration, and contempt, the latter being for my ignorance of his messianic missions and methods. His wife was frantic over her concern for him and fear for herself and young child. He would not accept treatment under any circumstances, insisting that it was his wife who needed psychiatric help. After having exhausted every technique of psychodynamics, support, and seduction at my command to instill some motivation for treatment in him, I commanded his hospitalization. With the authority of a field marshal, the inflexibility of a peace officer, and the sanction of a community whose little white suburban houses were being violated by the presence of someone so grossly disturbed, I had him hospitalized against his will. He had to be restrained by several guards and ambulance attendants when he became combative. After being tied to the stretcher, and as he was about to be taken out, he looked at me with cold anger and with the terrible perceptiveness of an unconscious laid bare to the world, he said, "You are regretting this already."

Regret! I had defined mental health as freedom and I was taking his away! Yes, I had all the justification, and yes, with my clinician's guidelines I would do the same thing under the same circumstances again. But how blinding it was to have the impure, red earth of human behavior thrown at my latest vision of a professional life.

I thought at first it was the recognition of hypocrisy that was keeping me awake. It was not. Hypocrisy is indifference to or nonrecognition of contradictions. What was going through me was the renewed, quickened, and urgent discovery that contradictions would always be with me. That, too, is absurd, that I should structure my activities so as to seek out contradictions.

However well or poorly the community psychiatrist does his job and with whatever degree of conspicuousness, the psychiatrist who devotes his efforts to social change will be looked upon as an absurd person. I mean this in both the superficial and existential senses of the word. In other words, he will be seen by some as the silliest, most ridiculous, and most contradictory of men, and by others as the most consistent and heroic. He will be called absurd because he will have voluntarily abrogated a sanctioned, if not revered, position in society, a stable and consistent and rational basis for practice and a firm and supportive brotherhood of peers for a whirlwind of irrationality and loneliness.

Social change is more than irrational. It is an irrational mixture of rational and irrational forces. The community psychiatrist in the arena of social change learns to accustom himself to having his values pulled from under him. The colleges he subscribes to are invisible ones, and he plays in a floating crap game of loose, informal, and ephemeral associations. He learns to live without sanction, for the rules he is constantly breaking are ones he may have helped to establish. He approaches his goal as the fox approaches his prey, in a circular, arbitrary, and flexible route always ready to change directions or indeed to change goals. The community psychiatrist engaged in social change invites ridicule because it is to invite ridicule to inquire into the meaning of life.

The most absurd aspect of social change, however, is that it is an exertion of all a man's will and strength in the face of hopelessness. The community psychiatrist finds himself sharing the ancient, endless burden of Sisyphus.

This book began with words of Albert Camus[1] and it will end with them:

> I have chosen this absurd and ineffectual effort. This is why I am on the side of the struggle. . . . The greatness has changed camp. It lies in protest and the blind alley sacrifice. There, too, it is not through a preference for defeat. Victory would be desirable. But there is but one victory, and it is eternal. That is the one I shall never have.

APPENDIX

The two following papers were prepared for other purposes but are presented here because they seem relevant to the subject matter of this book.

One paper is a brief description of a remarkable and optimistic development in urban ghettos across the Nation, a constructive reemergence and redefinition of the Negro gang. It was prepared at the request of the National Advisory Commission on Civil Disorders.

The second paper is a description of a model mental health program for the type of ghetto community generally chosen as the target area for a model cities' proposal to the Department of Housing and Urban Development. It was originally prepared for the Center for Community Planning of the Department of Health, Education and Welfare.

These papers present the type of input that a community psychiatrist can provide to the policies and programs which may have a tremendous impact on the mental health of large numbers of people.

148

THE ROLE OF YOUTH GROUPS IN THE
MINORITY COMMUNITY

We are witnessing a reemergence and redefinition of the "gang" in the Negro ghetto. The phenomenon of the inner-city group with its strict leadership and followership patterns, its uniforms, territoriality, and wars all but disappeared in the 50's. According to some, the gangs broke up because of the widespread use of heroin. According to others, police tactics, youth workers, and leadership co-option caused the disintegration of the gangs.

The epidemic use of heroin and the disappearance of gangs in the ghetto happened at the same time. In retrospect, people have suggested that gang membership provided an input of self-esteem, stimulation, and group identification which was otherwise absent and that heroin was used to fill the vacuum left by the disrupted groups. Even if this were true, however, it would be hard to idealize the gangs of the early 50's. The rivalries were deadly affairs with knives and zip-guns used to defend or attack turfs. Neighborhoods were terrorized by belligerent adolescents. Brutal beatings, thefts, and extortion were common. There were many deaths.

After a decade which witnessed the spread of heroin

addiction, the civil rights movement, antipovery legislation and summer rioting in rapid succession, the gangs are coming back. In many cases the old names persist: the Blackstone Rangers, The Disciples, Satans; in others, strange new names for Negro gangs: The Young Adults, Community Alert Patrol, The Real Great Society, and 12th and Oxford Filmmakers, Inc. They are gangs nonetheless.

Leadership is rigid and strictly enforced. Membership is not taken lightly: once a member, always a member. Territoriality is still a real phenomenon. The potential for violence persists and now heavier and more sophisticated weapons are available. On the other hand, there is less frequent resort to violence. More significant than this, however, is that some new gangs have taken a turn in the direction of community conservation, anti-crime, rehabilitation and counter-rioting activities, and have provided a basis for the development of Black business, cultural and political institutions.

The Blackstone Rangers control a major part of the Woodlawn community of Chicago. They have approximately 1800 members in the "Ranger Nation," as many as 1400 showing up for the weekly meetings in their headquarters at the First Presbyterian Church. They have a war cry, a uniform, and deadly weapons. They have a Pee-Wee Club for recruitment, a Rangerette Club for female companionship, and an aura of combined respect and fear in the community similar to that commanded by the Mafia in a Sicilian village. Children in Woodlawn do not play Cowboys and Indians; they play Rangers and Disciples. If you ask a young boy in the neighborhood what he wants to be when he grows up, he is likely to answer, "a Ranger."

The leaders of the Rangers are cloaked in the charisma, prestige and authority of folk heroes. They are probably responsible for a 25 percent reduction in the organized crime in Woodlawn. They have effectively prevented a riot in the area. They are being courted by political forces. They are signing treaties with other gangs. They are organizing business and getting grants. These things are happening in the face of an unremitting policy of harassment by a task force of the Chicago Police Department.

Their anti-crime activities have centered on the large-scale, syndicated activities in Woodlawn. The resort to narcotics (excluding marijuana) among gang members is severely punished. When a white man cruises along 63rd Street looking for a Negro prostitute, he is likely to be shown the way out of the community by a Ranger. Some members have suggested that one source of police hostility toward the gang may derive from a reduction in kickbacks to corrupt police officers as a result of the decline in syndicated crime.

The counter-riot activities of the gang also follow the two-pronged approach of controlling the behavior of the membership and influencing the community at large. During the riots on the West side of Chicago in the Lawndale area in 1966, the Ranger leadership called a "mandatory dance" of its membership every night of the disturbance. The Rangers also enforced a "voluntary curfew" in Woodlawn of anyone under the age of 25. By the use of a 24 hour a day telephone coverage system, they were able to convene a large number of Rangers anywhere in Woodlawn within 15 minutes to "cool" any group which threatened to riot.

More recently, when a congregation of young people

and a few smashed windows in Woodlawn threatened to spread, a leader of the Rangers shouted that anyone who wanted to die should be in the street in five minutes. Before five minutes had elapsed, the street was empty.

Another instance of the gang's control of community disorder took place during the January '67 blizzard that paralyzed the city for five days. While widespread looting of trucks was reported throughout the city, there was virtually no looting in the Woodlawn area due to the surveillance of the Rangers.

They are now called the Mighty Blackstone Rangers, Inc. and have become involved in the highly successful musical called *Opportunity Please Knock,* written by Oscar Brown, Jr., which was presented at the First Presbyterian Church and taken on the road to other cities. They have plans to open a restaurant and other similar small business ventures in Woodlawn.

The Blackstone Rangers is one example of what appears to be a spontaneous development in Negro ghettos across the country. Other examples are the Mission Rebels in Action in San Francisco, the Young Adults in Cleveland, the Community Alert Patrol and the Sons of Watts in Los Angeles, The Real Great Society in New York, the Rebels with a Cause in Washington, Satan's Disciples in Rochester and the 12th and Oxford Filmmakers, Inc., in Philadelphia.

There are characteristic patterns to these youth groups. Their membership is exclusively black. They are invariably school drop-outs with a background of thoroughgoing poverty and generally have police records. Their primary and often exclusive allegiance is to the gang or group.

They tend to use a Black Power rhetoric and are

suspicious or contemptuous of Caucasians and middle-class Negroes. They will often, however, accept alliances with one or a few trusted but endlessly tested whites and will not hesitate to enter into contractual arrangements with whites if they feel they are going to be advantaged. They will not tolerate being exploited for whatever purposes, ideological or otherwise. They consider the ghetto their home and could not care less about integration.

They are very aware of efforts to co-opt their leaders and they resent these efforts as their leaders resist them. The leadership itself tends to fall into an executive role constellation with a group of individuals at the top. At least three types are seen: the fighter, the planner, and the image bearer. The last tends to be a handsome and charismatic person, nominally the head of the group but relying on the planner's intellect and the fighter's strength to maintain control. As a group and as individuals, they are not afraid of violence.

What are the implications of this development?

The nature and functions of these organizations tend to confirm the findings of Nathan Caplan in his studies of the Detroit riot scene. Caplan found that the psychosocial profile of the rioter is closer to that of the counter-rioter than either is to the non-rioter. Apparently the line between destructive and constructive activism is much finer than the line between activism itself and passivity. Significant from a psychological point of view is that the rioter-counter-rioter group tends to see the environment as responsive to the efforts of individuals rather than individuals being the passive objects of environmental forces.

There is broad agreement among psychiatrists that a crucial element of mental health is a sense of environmental mastery, a feeling that some part of the cosmos, however small, is subject to the control and manipulation of the individual.

With this in mind, one may have to conclude that the rioter is a more mentally healthy person than the non-rioter. He is a person who still believes that action means something, that things can improve. I am not, of course, implying that a riot is simply an activist social protest demonstration. It is a mixture of forces—some destructive and suicidal—and others, just as salient, which are expressions of hope and initiative.

This brings to mind DeTocqueville's statement about the French Revolution. He said, "The French rebelled when their situation improved. The evil became unendurable when it was no longer perceived as inevitable."

This may help to explain why Negro rioting appeared on the American scene after the civil rights movement and antipoverty legislation. It may also help explain why such relatively competent and progressive cities as Detroit and New Haven have had riots. The riots, themselves, may be evidence that we were going in the right direction, but not quite fast enough.

This theoretical position, in conjunction with the empirical history of ghetto youth groups, leads one to believe that the same individuals can at one time participate in rioting and at another be part of a conservative and business-minded movement. Moynihan's picture of the rioters as an anomic under-class, a lumpenproletariat, does not fit with the facts. It was the already urbanized, Northern Negro who rioted—not the uprooted recent in-migrant—confused, helpless and hopeless.

Depending on the forces brought to play upon them,

the aggressive energies of the new gangs may be channelled into a revitalized, decentralized, community based capitalism or they may reemerge as pure rage.

The new youth groups in the ghettos may do more for America than control rioting and become Black business associations. They may provide a model for something that is even more desperately needed—adolescent institutions. At a time in history when minority groups are demanding a piece of the action, some control over their own destinies, we have completely ignored the needs of youth itself. Unlike Holland, which has the Provos, and Yugoslavia, which has a youth-administered national recreation program, the United States has no example of institutions organized by and for the young. We have guarded our precious institutions from youth until youth becomes what we unthinkingly call maturity. Without referring to what this has done to our institutions, let me merely suggest that it has wreaked havoc with the young. Like any deprived group, they have become resentful and suspicious and have spent their vitality in unconstructive pursuits.

It is a little ironic that while the Rangers, Community Alert Patrol and The Real Great Society are demonstrating what adolescent can do as entrepreneurs, law enforcers and political activists, the white, middle-class adolescent is afforded no such opportunity and turns to distorted consciousness, promiscuity, and a nihilistic ideology to sustain himself. As a model for alternative courses, the ghetto youth gangs may prove to be the saving grace of white, middle-class life.

A MODEL COMMUNITY MENTAL HEALTH
PROGRAM FOR A MODEL CITIES AREA

If we were to think of mental health in its broadest sense, as something positive with elements of freedom, integrity, and environmental mastery, then the entire model cities program is itself a mental health program. The final common path of the physical and social reconstruction of an urban community is the enhancement of the quality of life of the individuals within it.

On the other hand, even if mental health is more than the absence of mental illness, no program can hope to be successful if it ignores individuals already suffering from such disorders. There is abundant evidence that the poverty-stricken, segregated, mobile, and disorganized people who inhabit the communities selected as model city areas have higher rates of mental illness than any other population in the United States.

The planning and implementing of a model cities program provides an ideal opportunity for a city to organize a comprehensive and coordinated community mental health program for its most needy citizens. I hope to provide a model for such a program in this paper. I want to emphasize that while this model has certain idealized aspects to it, there is nothing fanciful or utopian about it. Every component outlined below has been demonstrated in one locale or another. More importantly, the construction, staffing, and coordination of these components is feasible through the existing grant mechanisms of the National Institute of Mental Health.

One thing more needs particular emphasis. A coordinated mental health program is coordinated externally as well as internally. Not only are the elements within it integrated and complementary, but also the entire mental health program must be integrated with and complementary to every other component of the model cities program. With this in mind, the first recommendation is that a mental health professional, and preferably the program director of the involved community mental health center, be a board member of the City Development Agency.

The model area mental health program is conceptualized along three parameters—prevention, treatment, and rehabilitation.

Preventive Programs: The purpose of preventive mental health programs is to reduce the incidence of mental disorders. This is to be achieved in the model area by the implementation of two broad activities; one is *community organization* and the other is the establishment of a network of *mental health consultation.*

The community organization program may be undertaken independently by the mental health program or be in conjunction with other community organization efforts in the model area. The latter is preferable from the point of view of assuring coordination with other model area programs, but some community organization staff should be in the employ of the mental health program. The community organization activity is geared to identifying organized groups in the community who have an interest in mental health and to convening conferences and meetings with them. This provides an input into the mental health program of information about unmet community needs and desires. It also provides a reciprocal channel of communication back to these groups of the perceptions and plans of the mental health professionals.

More important to the preventive aspect, the community organization efforts will be directed toward the development of neighborhood and community groups among the as yet unaffiliated and disorganized people in the area: welfare recipients, public housing residents, tenement dwellers, the hard-core poor who have the most severe and the most extensive psychological and social pathology. This activity will hope to demonstrate to the target population that the mental health program is responsive to their needs and is, in fact, their program. It will also serve to increase the sense of community and environmental mastery, to reduce the helplessless, hopelessness, anomie, and alienation that this population is heir to. Community organization, then, is not merely a means of making more meaningful and useful a mental health program, but is itself a major mental health service, an end in itself.

Community organization efforts, to be successful, must be oriented around specific realizable goals. For the model area mental health program, at least two such goals will provide the foci of the C.O. activities. One is the recruitment of the nonprofessionals working in the program and the other is the development of a broadly representative Model Area Community Mental Health Board in which will reside final policy and budgetary responsibility.

Mental health consultation to other community institutions holds, of course, the promise that individuals with mental disorders who are involved with these institutions may be found early. But a more basically preventive aspect of consultation is the provision of the knowledge, skill or objectivity about mental health concerns to other community agents so that they may perform their own assigned functions in a way that most enhances the mental health of their clients. The policies and practices of every agency that deals with people may be benefited by such consultation, whether their functions are teaching, job placement, law enforcement or religion; the practitioners will be able to perform more effectively if their sophistication about and sensitivity to people's problems could be increased through regular contacts with mental health consultants.

Among the consumer agencies for such a program might be welfare departments, civil rights organizations, community action programs, job placement centers, unions, large employers, public health departments, courts and corrections departments, vocational rehabilitation agencies, police departments, schools, settlement houses, recreation programs, churches, youth gangs and taverns.

An agency that should be singled out as a prime target for consultation is the relocation authority, which will have extensive responsibilities in the model city area. Relocation is a mental health crisis of major proportions and, as with every crisis, opportunities as well as hazards to mental health exist.

The community organizations will be most effective if they are not cloistered in a central facility, but are dispersed and decentralized throughout the area. Their most effective base of operations might then be store-front neighborhood service centers dispersed throughout the community.

The consultation program can be coordinated and administered out of the central office of the community mental health center.

Treatment: To meet the needs of the target population, the treatment programs in the model area must be (1) immediately responsive to salient problems, (2) accessible, (3) pluralistic in its approach and (4) unencumbered by the traditional, middle-class psychiatric model of passivity, reserve and selectivity.

Psychiatric outpatient treatment programs have generally excluded from care the types of patients who inhabit the model area. Psychotherapy has been the major treatment modality, and, as commonly practiced, this requires a patient who is verbal, insightful, motivated for treatment, capable of delaying gratification, and who more or less shares the values of the therapist. In short, psychotherapy has been a middle-class treatment for middle-class patients. The techniques and the methods of delivering treatment will have to be modified for the model area. The mechanisms for this have already been demonstrated. Rather than being located in a distant, austere and impersonal facility, the first line of outpatient treatment resources should be in *neighborhood, store-front facilities.* These should be comfortable, convenient and informal. *Indigenous nonprofessional personnel* will be utilized not only for such amenities as serving coffee and watching children, but as intake workers and, with appropriate training and supervision, as mental health aides carrying out a major role in the treatment program. Counselling, educational and supportive interventions are more effective for such populations when provided by carefully selected, trained and supervised people who emerge from that population. They provide bridges between the expertise of the mental health professionals and the inarticulate, impatient needs of the model area.

For more severe or subtle emotional problems, social workers, psychologists and psychiatrists should be available for diagnosis, casework, group work, psychotherapy and drug treatment.

The emphasis in psychotherapy should be on short-term, individual, group or family techniques with crisis resolution rather than personality restructuring as the goal. There should be no waiting lists for treatment.

Since it cannot be expected that a working class population has the option of taking time off during a 9 to 5 working day, treatment should be available during evenings or Saturdays.

For psychiatric emergencies such as potential suicides, acute anxiety states or acute psychiatric reactions, immediate psychiatric evaluation and disposition should be available. As these so often require general medical, as well as psychiatric attention, such situations should be dealt with in the *emergency unit* of a general hospital or comprehensive health center. Emergency psychiatric care must be available seven days a week, twenty-four hours a day.

When a psychiatric patient requires greater scrutiny or more elaborate treatment than can be provided in an outpatient setting, he may be hospitalized in a short stay *inpatient unit* of the general hospital or mental health center for twenty-four hour care or *day, night or evening hospital care.* In the latter facility, the patient either spends his days on the unit, returning home to sleep or spends his evenings and/or nights at the hospital and works during the day. The idea here is to avoid the stigma, dependency and social isolation of unnecessarily extensive or prolonged hospitalization.

If long term hospitalization is necessary, the closest *state hospital* may be the only recourse. In order to minimize the psychological distance, sense of defeat and possible social breakdown effects of state hospitalization, there should be a unit of the hospital devoted exclusively to residents of the model area with a staff that rotates with the community treatment program.

Discharge from this unit should be planned from the day of admission with follow-up in the day or night center, or the store front center, or a halfway house, and should be facilitated for every patient.

A home visiting service should be available for individual and family problems of an acute or chronic nature where the people involved are unwilling or unable to reach a standing mental health facility. The home visiting service may be the major component of a *suicide prevention* program where would-be suicides may be visited immediately if need be after a call to the *centralized information and triage service* has been placed.

Specialized treatment programs for narcotics addicts, alcoholics or psychedelic emergencies can be incorporated into the above network of facilities. *A detoxification unit* under joint psychiatric and medical control should be available at the general hospital or comprehensive health center.

Rehabilitation: Rehabilitation efforts will be directed towards reducing the functional incapacities of the mentally ill in the model area. The line between treatment and rehabilitation programs is obviously an arbitrary one in that each of the activities has elements in common with the other and is meaningless without the other. The emphasis in rehabilitation, however, is on the severely and chronically disordered individuals, the chronic schizophrenic, the character disorder, the addict and the mentally retarded.

The three major rehabilitation components in the model area will be an *industrial activities program,* a *foster care program* and a network of *halfway houses.*

Chronic psychiatric patients, addicts, derelict alcoholics and retardates invariably require vocational training and placement in order to make an adequate social adjustment without institutional care. An office of the *state vocational rehabilitation agency* should be located within the model area and have close liaison with the community mental health program. The vocational rehabilitation agency can provide evaluation, training, placement and counseling services for such individuals. Regular and intensive administrative and case consultation from a mental health professional is mandatory. The mental health consultant can also be a linkage person providing reciprocal referrals and information between the agencies.

Consultation and education activities with *unions and large employers* will help pave the way for an incorporation of mentally ill patients into private industry. Regardless of how successful that is, however, there will be a need for *sheltered workshops* where individuals without the social or personal skills to make it in a competitive, profit oriented atmosphere can still be engaged in productive and remunerative activities. This can be provided by the Salvation Army or Goodwill Industries, but if such workshops are inadequate for sufficient numbers of patients, then a workshop administered by the mental health program itself can be utilized. Such activities have been found to be self-supporting, as with a nonprofit orientation they can competitively bid for contracts.

Labor unions will have to be educated about the necessity and value of such programs so that they do not misconstrue them as exploitative or threatening to the unions.

Chronically ill or retarded individuals have been found to function more satisfactorily in the *homes of selected, supervised and paid families* than in most institutions. There have been very dramatic instances of "social recovery" in such a setting. Elderly couples or individuals who themselves cannot get work, but are not disabled, very often provide a wholesome and warm environment, a nurturing atmosphere for children and adults who hunger for such an atmosphere. At the same time, the aging foster parents (or foster grandparents) are involved in an activity that provides them with a sense of purpose, importance and commitment.

Mothers obtaining welfare aid who are competent and patient child-rearers and who prefer to remain with their children rather than work outside the home may also be interested in having an emotionally disturbed or retarded youngster under their responsibility.

It is important to provide adequate compensation to foster parents to increase motivation and underline the importance of their function.

The recruitment and supervision for such placements can best be undertaken by the *home visiting service,* which will make regular and frequent visits to each foster home.

For individuals who do not require hospitalization or close medical scrutiny but who are not yet able to be independent and for whom foster care is unavailable or inappropriate, a *halfway house* can provide the bridge back to society. This is a community-based house, looking like any other in the neighborhood, where a dozen or so people may sleep, eat and commune while they are finding jobs or undergoing treatment. The atmosphere should be one of a humane boarding house with a sophisticated and sensitive staff, rather than any kind of institution. This may be under the direction of the mental health program, or self-help organizations such as *Synanon, A.A.,* or *Recovery, Inc.,* may be invited to establish their facilities in the model area.

Figures 1, 2 and 3 provide a summary outline of the preventive, treatment and rehabilitation components of the model area mental health program. All of these program elements should be available but the specific personnel, structural and administrative mechanisms for carrying them out will vary with the resources and resourcefulness of the model areas.

The existence of these elements is not enough. They must be tied together as cohesive, interdependent entities. Their staffs must have a primary allegiance to the superordinate goal of the entire model city program, the total welfare of the community.

A university affiliation is desirable for all aspects of this mental health program. It would promise high standards of treatment and training and also be a locus of objective and qualified research and evaluation activities. However, a university is frequently looked upon as an alien or academically parasitic force in typical model city areas. To insure against the university's adopting a condescending or cavalier attitude toward the community, the specifics of its involvement must be subject to the *control of the community*.

That this mental health program is in fact under the control of the community must be the overriding principal of its planning and activities. This may involve tensions with the professionals participating in it as their conception of standards may at times be compromised by the manifest desires of the community. If the professionals are unable to educate the representatives of the community about the efficacy and value of their ideas, then it should be those ideas rather than the community's control of the program that should be compromised.

Figure 1:

PREVENTION

Community Organization:
- Coordination of established groups
- Development of new community groups

Consultation and Education:
- Welfare
- Relocation Authority
- Schools
- Public Health
- Civil Rights Groups
- Community Action Program
- Job Placement Centers
- Vocational Rehabilitation Agency
- Police
- Courts and Corrections
- Settlement Houses
- Churches
- Gangs
- Taverns

Figure 2:

TREATMENT
Information & Triage via 24-hour/7-day week Telephone service

Outpatient
Diagnosis
Counsel
Support
Psychotherapy: individual, group, family
Casework
Drug Treatment
— Store Front Centers

Emergency
Evaluation
Treatment
— Emergency Ward of General Hospital
— Home Visiting Service

Short-stay Hospitalization
24-hour/day, night, evening
Detoxification for Alcoholics and drug abusers
— Inpatient Unit
General Hospital
Community Mental Health Center
Comprehensive Health Center

Long-stay Hospitalization
— Model Area Unit at State Hospital

Evaluation and treatment of individuals unwilling or unable to attend other facilities
— Home Visiting Service

Figure 3:

REHABILITATION

Industrial programs:
{ Consultation with unions and employers
Liaison with state vocational rehabilitation agency
Sheltered workshops

Foster Family Care:
{ With aged individuals and couples (controlled by the home visiting service)
With mothers on A.F.D.C.

Halfway Houses:
{ Mental Health Facility
A.A., Synanon, and similar

REFERENCES AND ANNOTATIONS

THE GENESIS OF A COMMUNITY
PSYCHIATRIST

1

1. There has yet to be an epidemiological survey that does not demonstrate an inverse relationship between socioeconomic class and mental illness. The three most significant studies in the past decade showing how the poor tend to have more psychopathology are those by Leighton, Hollingshead and Redlich, and Rennie and Srole et al (Leighton, A. H., et al, *Sterling County Study of Psychiatric Disorder and Sociocultural Environment*, Vol. I, II, and III, New York, Basic Books, 1959. Hollingshead, A. B., and Redlich, F. C., *Social Class and Mental Illness: A Community Study*, New York, Wiley, 1958. Rennie, T. A. C., Srole, L., et al, *Mental Health in the Metropolis*, New York, McGraw-Hill, 1962). There continue to be arguments that the relationship is an artifact of downward social mobility secondary to mental illness itself. While there can be no doubt that this does occur and that it explains some of the correlation, the data from New Haven about the "incidence" of mental illness, i.e., new case rates as well as the data from the Midtown Study about the socio-economic status of the *parents* of interviewees, suggests that there is more to the relation between poverty and mental illness than downward mobility. For a succinct overview of the interface between mental illness and poverty, see Greenblatt, M., Emery, P., and Glueck, B., *Poverty and Mental Health*, Psychiatric Research Report No. 22, American Psychiatric Association, Washington, D.C., 1967. For a more exhaustive and scholarly

volume on the same interface, see *Mental Health of the Poor: New Treatment Approaches for Low Income People,* edited by Frank Riessman, Jerome Cohen, and Arthur Pearl, New York, The Free Press, 1964. One of our major conceptual problems is, of course, that we do not really know what we mean by "poverty." We can operationally define "social class" as most surveyors do in terms of housing, employment, education, and like factors, but there continue to be debates as to whether there actually exists a "culture of poverty" on which we can blame all the deprivations we instinctively associate with being "poor." See the works of Oscar Lewis, *The Children of Sanchez, Autobiography of a Mexican Family,* New York, Random House, 1961, and of Hylan Lewis, "Culture, Class and the Behavior of Low Income Families," paper presented at Conference on Views of Lower Class Culture, New York, N.Y., June 27, 1963, for the two sides of this debate. To complicate the picture even more, Leighton has made it plain that the socio-cultural disintegration he finds correlated with mental illness is not exclusively associated with poverty. He describes the same phenomenon as an occurrence associated with the sudden assumption of affluence by a community.

2. Rudolf Virchow, "The Father of Pathology," and one of the great names in the history of medicine, while investigating a typhus epidemic in Upper Silesia, said that while it was quite likely that there was an agent as yet unidentified in this disease, the way to eliminate typhus was to eliminate poverty, overcrowding and lack of adequate food. Virchow also once said, "Medicine is nothing but a social science. Politics is nothing but medicine on a large scale." As another indication of his breadth of vision, in 1849 he wrote:

In reality, if medicine is the science of the healthy as
well as of the ill human being (which is what it ought
to be), what other science is better suited to prepare
laws as the basis of the social structure, in order to
make effective those which are inherent in man himself? Once medicine is established in anthropology,
and once the interests of the privileged no longer
determine the course of public events, the physiologist
and the practitioner will be counted among the elder
statesmen who support the social structure. Medicine
is a social science in its very bone and marrow. . . .

This can be found along with other insights of this
remarkable man in *Disease, Life and Man, Selected Es-
says by Rudolf Virchow,* translated and introduced by
Helfand Rather, Stanford, California, Stanford University
Press, 1958.

3. This refers to the well-known Stanton and
Schwartz effect described by these authors in *The Mental
Hospital,* Stanton, A. H., and Schwartz, M. S., New York,
Basic Books, 1954. The book is subtitled "A Study of
Institutional Participation in Psychiatric Illness and Treatment." It is one of the earliest discoveries (or rediscoveries)
of the profound impact of the milieu on the sickness and
health of psychiatric patients. Among the origins of this
renaissance of social psychiatry, however, have to be considered the observations made during World War II and
the Korean War about the relationships between duration
of illness and such factors as rapid discharge from hospital,
community- (in this case, field-) based treatment, and close-
ness to peers. My own early experience with milieu phenomena was as a medical student at the University of
Chicago when I participated in a study concerning the
impact of decision-making on a psychiatric ward. For a

description of this superficial, but, to me, convincing study, see "Patient and Staff Reactions to a Change in Procedure on a Psychiatric Ward," Dumont, M. P., Daniels, R. S., Margolis, P. M., Carson, R. C., and Ham, J., in *Diseases of the Nervous System*, Vol. XXI, No. 4, April, 1960.

4. Dumont, M. P., and Aldrich, C. K., "Family Care After a Thousand Years—a Crisis in the Tradition of St. Dymphna," *The American Journal of Psychiatry*, Vol. CXIX, No. 2, August, 1962. The American Medical Association Film Library has an amateurish and barely intact film, *The Geel Colony, a Thousand Years of Family Care* (No. P41, American Medical Association, Chicago, photography by H. Rademacker), which I wrote, edited, and narrated. It shows the "malades" of Geel working, relaxing, and living in a completely integrated way with the normal townspeople.

5. Ernest Gruenberg has written an excellent re-evaluation and definition of this syndrome in an article, "The Social Breakdown Syndrome—Some Origins," *The American Journal of Psychiatry*, Vol. CXXIII, No. 12, June, 1967.

6. Bateson, G., Jackson, D. D., Haley, J., and Weakland, J., "Towards a Theory of Schizophrenia," *Behavioral Science*, Vol. I, No. 251, 1956.

7. Berne, Eric, *Games People Play*, New York, Grove Press, 1964. Dr. Berne tends to see his family-oriented transactional therapy as a preparation for more traditional psychoanalytic therapy of individuals. Other family therapists have the courage of Dr. Berne's convictions. There is a broad spectrum of attitudes among family therapists including that of Erika Chance (*Families in Treatment*, New York, Basic Books, 1959), who, while talking of pa-

tient-families, really sees the impact of therapy on the child and focuses outcome evaluations on intrapersonal changes. Virginia Satir (*Conjoint Family Therapy,* Palo Alto, California, Science and Behavior Books, 1964) shifts the emphasis away from the identified patient as the focus of treatment; however, she sees the pained marital relationship as the origin of pathology and so narrows down on the husband-wife duality in her interventions. At the farthest extreme are the most transactional of family therapists. Nathan Ackerman (*The Psychodynamics of Family Life,* New York, Basic Books, 1958) states, "The family is the basic unit of growth and experience, fulfillment or failure. It is also the basic unit of illness and health." He actually sees the process of family therapy as a reprojection of intrapsychic conflict into a field of family interaction. As another example of this perspective on family therapy, Lyman Wynne (in his chapter "Intrafamilial Alignments and Splits," in *Exploring the Base for Family Therapy,* Ackerman et al, New York, Family Service Association of America, 1961) wrote:

> The distinctive principles and problems of 'exploratory' family therapy . . . rest upon the assumption that the 'patient,' the subject of the family therapy, is not an individual or an aggregate of individuals meeting to talk about an individual, but is the interlocking system of family relationships.

And, finally, Sanford Sherman (in his chapter "Exploring the Base for Family Therapy," in *Exploring the Base for Family Therapy,* Ackerman et al, New York, Family Service Association of America, 1961) said:

> Changing from family-oriented diagnosis and treatment to family diagnosis and treatment is more than

an increase in intensity of the same approach. It represents a shift to viewing the distress of the individual as less the problem than a symptom of the problem of pathology in the whole family.

THE SOUND OF ONE HAND CLAPPING

2

1. Gerald Caplan's work (*Principles of Preventive Psychiatry*, New York, Basic Books, 1964) is the major attempt to date to develop a conceptual scheme for community psychiatry. It is based primarily on public health ideas and a theory of crisis intervention.

2. For a beautifully written description of the confluence of the tenets of Zen Buddhism and Western psychiatry, see *Psychotherapy, East and West*, by Alan Watts (New York, Pantheon Books, 1961). Watts was probably not aware of newer "transactional" ideas in psychiatry nor of community psychiatry in general, which demonstrate more striking parallels to Zen thinking.

3. For a rich and wise discussion of these issues, see Thomas Mann's introduction to his magnum opus, *Joseph and His Brothers* (New York, Knopf, 1948). He discusses whether or not Joseph's father, Jacob, is really the son of Isaac, the wrestler of angels. Historically, Joseph's being Isaac's grandson does not seem likely, and for contemporary Western sensibilities this immediate generational link seems impossible. Mann, however, conveys the subtle idea that for Joseph's father the collective identity as the

bearer of the Hebrew lineage is more important than biological individuality. It matters little whether Isaac was the grandfather of Joseph or a more distant relation. Jacob was the Jacob of Abraham and Isaac and always will be whether or not he was their direct scion.

4. At a certain level of abstraction, the history of ideas provides a miraculous and exquisitely beautiful image of the essential harmony of all profound insights. The confluence of Zen Buddhism ("the self does not exist"), European Existentialism ("existence precedes essence"), and American Pragmatism ("possibilities exceed actuality") is one such image. It would take a good deal more than a footnote to tie these philosophical currents together in terms of their implications for mental health.

WHAT IS MENTAL HEALTH?

3

1. Mark Van Doren once said that it is a sign of a great work of literature that nothing written about it is so interesting as the work itself. I wonder if this isn't also true of a brilliant philosophical insight. The storm of controversy that Hannah Arendt's book *Eichmann in Jerusalem: A Report on the Banality of Evil*, New York, Viking Press, 1964, caused is not nearly so interesting or illuminating as that book itself. One can certainly understand why it caused such a controversy. It would be so much more comfortable for us to believe that the crimes of the Nazis were peculiar to a few deranged arch-criminals

rather than being an expression of a universal capacity for bureaucratized brutality. An outraged civilization felt it could rest easy after executing the likes of Eichmann, as if the world were cleaner, more wholesome, and freer now.

2. Obviously I have been influenced by the writings of Erich Fromm, particularly his *Escape from Freedom* (New York, Farrar and Rinehart, 1941) and *The Sane Society* (New York, Rinehart, 1955). The best overview of psychiatric perspectives on mental health are in *Current Concepts of Positive Mental Health,* by Marie Jahoda (New York, Basic Books, 1958). She finds six overriding principles of mental health in current psychiatric parlance: environmental mastery, attitudes towards the self, self-actualization, integration, autonomy, and perception of reality.

THE CITY AS PATIENT

4

1. Elliot Liebow in *Tally's Corner* (Boston, Little, Brown, 1967) gives a vivid description of the style of life and perceptions of lower class Negro men standing around on the street corners of the ghetto. The writer is an example of a new breed of social scientist: committed to contemporary urban problems, concerned with the implications of knowledge, and sensitive to people as people rather than as subjects. For another picture of what it is like—in a somewhat more literary vein—try *Manchild*

in the Promised Land by Claude Brown (New York, Signet, 1965). Even a government report, amazingly enough, which was prepared with integrity and utilizing the voices of ghetto residents themselves, tells it as it is: the Civil Rights Commission's report, *A Time to Listen . . . A Time to Act,* released November, 1967, under the staff direction of William L. Taylor. An occasional film communicates with sensitivity and accuracy the quality of life in the ghetto. A CBS documentary, *The Tenement,* describing life in and around one building on the South Side of Chicago, is masterful. An erstwhile fighting gang in Philadelphia, now known as the 12th and Oxford Film-makers, Inc., made a twenty-minute film called *The Jungle,* which tells of the need for stimulation and group identification that leads toward gang membership and street wars. But films, novels, government reports, and anthropological case studies are no substitute for the real thing. You have to smell the garbage, hear the rats, see the decay, and listen to a firsthand encounter with a brutal cop, an indignant welfare worker, an impatient rent man or an exploiting businessman to get the full impact.

    2. For breathtaking documentation of this, see *The Wretched of the Earth,* by Frantz Fanon (New York, Grove Press, 1966). The book is by a Negro psychoanalyst in Algeria who writes about anticolonial and antiracist struggles throughout the world. This book has become a handbook for militant Black Power ideologies in this country.

    3. Leo Tolstoy, *Resurrection,* New York, Oxford, 1952. For some reason Tolstoy's last novel is not very popular in this country. It is probably a bit too moralistic,

even by Tolstoy's standards, but it is still extraordinarily subtle, and its message is pertinent to contemporary liberalism, as, I suppose, it always will be.

4. Byrd, R. E., *Alone*, New York, Putnam, 1938. We did not know very much about sensory deprivation psychosis when this book was written, but it is a firsthand description of such an episode.

5. Hollingshead, A. B., and Rogler, L. H., "Attitudes Toward Slums and Public Housing in Puerto Rico," in Leonard J. Duhl, editor, *The Urban Condition*, New York, Basic Books, 1963. This study describes a survey of families matched for age, socio-economic status, marital union and area of residence and differentiated by presence of mental illness. It was primarily a study of schizophrenia in the lower class, but the salient finding was that while families in modern, clean, inexpensive public housing disliked their neighborhoods, the residents of decrepit, unhealthy, and relatively expensive slums liked theirs—evidently because of a greater sense of community in the slum.

6. Fried, M., "Grieving for a Lost Home," in Leonard J. Duhl, editor, *The Urban Condition*, New York, Basic Books, 1963. The results of the massive and highly significant West End Study in Boston will soon be made public. This article focuses on the sense of loss experienced by relocatees from the West End—which is indistinguishable from an acute grief reaction. The studies were initiated by Dr. Erich Lindemann, then the Chairman, Department of Psychiatry, Massachusetts General Hospital, and were an attempt to fit sociological data into his theory of crisis. The results were more dramatic than anyone expected. As one relocatee put it, "Something of me went with the West End."

7. Dumont, M. P., "Death of the Leader in a Therapy Group of Schizophrenics," *The International Journal of Group Psychotherapy*, Vol. XVI, No. 2, April, 1966.

8. Chronologies of riots will unhappily become commonplace before too long. The best portrait of a riot situation to date, however, with detailed, minute by minute documentation of what happened along with an analysis of immediate and longer term precipitants is in *Years of Darkness, Rivers of Blood,* by Robert Conat, New York, Bantam Books, 1967. It describes the 1965 riot in South Central Los Angeles, and illuminates the roles of the police, the National Guard, and the mass media during the uprising as well as courtroom activities afterwards. Of particular relevance to this discussion of environmental mastery are the descriptions of exhilaration, at times almost ecstasy, on the part of participants in the riot who for the first time in their lives saw the police and the rest of the city's establishment reacting to them as if they had importance and power. Los Angeles, like the rest of the country, has not learned that the sense of importance and power that emerged during the holocaust was not otherwise available to rioters.

9. Donald Michael is a brilliant and perceptive futurist at the Institute for Social Research at the University of Michigan. He combines a sophistication about technology and social psychology and an ability to perceive salient trends. His analysis of the impact of a shift to long-range planning in urban life is in process. For an example of his work, see *The Next Generation,* New York, Vintage Books, 1963.

10. An apocalyptic glimpse into the future of automation and its implications for the Protestant Ethic was

given by Lawrence C. Murdock, Jr., Vice President and Secretary of the Federal Reserve Bank of Philadelphia in a speech to the 1967 Adirondack Workshop of the National Social Welfare Assembly, entitled "Will Abundance Be Our Undoing?"

11. The controversy that followed in the wake of the Moynihan Report (*The Negro Family—The Case for National Action,* United States Department of Labor, 1965) provides the converse of what I said about Hannah Arendt's book on Eichmann. In this case, the discussions of the work are every bit as interesting as the report itself. See *The Moynihan Report and the Politics of Controversy,* by Rainwater, L., and Yancey, W., Cambridge, Massachusetts, M.I.T. Press, 1967. To add my own two cents to the controversy I would suggest that Moynihan was not really writing about the Negro family but about the white family in the Negro community. What I mean is that Moynihan was not speaking from an anthropological or even an astute sociological perspective on Negro family life but was analyzing census data and drawing inferences based on a normative standard of white middle-class family structure. It is possible, though not yet demonstrated, that the Negro family is based on a pattern of fictive family relationships with "play fathers" who are actually part of an extended family that is as stable and supportive of individual development as the standard white middle-class family. What was so offensive to the Negro community was the implication, undoubtedly unintended, in the report that the problems of the Black Man were somehow the result of his own inadequacy. . . . The report might have avoided such an implication by emphasizing that a program of full employment and desegregation was being

suggested rather than a saturation program of case services geared to repairing defective child-rearing practices.

12. For a picture of how the Nation is prepared to deal with the symptom of rioting, see "The Second Civil War" by Gary Wills in *Esquire Magazine,* March, 1968, Vol. LXIX, No. 3. The article is a restrained but awesome description of the preparations by police departments for another summer of violence and the reciprocal preparations by ghetto militants. The image is of two massive juggernauts heading toward one another with increasing momentum. The process is one of mobilization for imminent, and as a result, inevitable, war. The components of this mobilization appear to me to be at least three in number.

The first is a process of polarization. The lines are being drawn more and more tightly. There seems to be no buffer zone, no neutralizing force, and certainly no bridge building. The white liberals and the Negro middle class are being forced to choose sides. In an early morning conversation made intimate by whiskey, the brooding sounds of the nearby Pacific surf and the presence of a dark-skinned woman who was beautiful and grave in her rapt attention, a brilliant and sensitive Negro social scientist, known as a spokesman for social justice for several more decades than I have been alive, talked about his son. His son had felt a growing sense of alliance with the militant voices from the ghetto demanding retribution. His son had said, "I am ready to shoot a honky." The Negro scientist shook his head slowly and said, "I don't know what to say to him."

I have heard the same dismay from the fathers of hippies. But what a difference. The hippie says to his father, "You have failed me. I want to love." The militant says to his father, "You have failed me. I want to hate." Those of us in the white world who are cursed or blessed with hippie children may be humane and open-minded enough to listen to what they are saying. We can't be appalled when we do. Their message is as light and noble as it is ancient. The poignancy and tragedy of the polarization by race in the city is that along with the assertion of pride and power of the militants is a burden of hatred. It is understandable, and, by a talion instinct, it is just, but it is no less a burden.

On the other side, the white liberal is being forced into the ranks of the brutal, thoughtless authoritarians. He finds himself in the company of an outraged and panicked lower-middle class, armed to the teeth and prepared to kill. The content of the liberal's thought, his programs of social reform, are trampled upon by racists—anger, impatience, inflexibility on both sides. He is left only with the process of his thought, an insubstantial wisp called criticism. The programs of liberalism can seek allies and choose strategies and tactics. The process of liberalism cannot. It is always on the grandstand watching and with sadness anticipating the casualties from the playing out of social forces. Criticism will not shield the liberal from the brickbats of either the revolutionary Blacks or the counterrevolutionary Whites. He will have to choose sides or be among the first casualties.

The Negro middle class and the white liberal had barely clasped hands; now they are being thrust apart by violent and inhumane forces—the color line. Du Bois was right, it is *the* problem of the 20th Century.

The second component of this massive, domestic mobilization for civil war is a *sense of righteousness*. On both sides is rhetoric. The White world will uphold "law and

order" and the Black world will demand retribution. On
the one hand we hear "lawlessness cannot be condoned,"
"the social order will be maintained." On the other hand
we hear the demand for "justice for the Black man," "re-
venge for White crimes," "reparations for inequities."

Emerging from these righteous cries on both sides is
the third component of this imminent war, a *legitimization of violence*. "Law and order" will be maintained at
any cost and the revolutionary demands for "justice" will
be upheld at any cost. The costs are counted in lives.

Why are these three elements, polarization, righteousness, and the legitimization of violence present? We already know the underlying reasons but why are they present now with such ferocity and irrevocability? From what
does this war mentality come?

How hard do we have to look to see the obvious? A
war mentality comes from war. The more brutal the war,
the more brutalizing. Every act of violence carries within
it the seeds of subsequent acts of violence. Our nation is
engaged in an orgy of violence in South East Asia and
each death nurtures the origins of a thousand more. It is
like a gigantic act of procreation where violent death gen-
erates still more violent death. We are about to experience
the blood-lust in our own cities. Polarization, righteousness
and legitimized violence are transposed with facility from
the streets of Saigon to the streets of Detroit.

The war in Vietnam and the war in our cities are
locking into place along contiguous ideological lines. Militant voices from the ghetto see the war in Asia as a racist
one. They see it as the destruction of "colored people."
With or without justice, they insist that such a war would
not be fought in Europe against a white enemy. On the
other side, militant whites see the Black Power movement

as a Red movement. With whatever justice or lack of it they see Marxist, Mao-ist and Che-ist ideologues behind the Black militant ideology. They are prepared to believe that money and arms flow from Peking to the ghettos of America.

We know from studies in Detroit and Newark that disproportionate numbers of returned Negro veterans from the Vietnamese war have been involved as rioters during the uprisings.

We know that weapons and anti-guerrilla tactics developed for the war in Asia are being developed for use against Black rioters in our cities.

We know that many youths in the ghetto between the ages of 13 and 17 see only two alternatives open to them: being killed in Vietnam or getting arrested to avoid being drafted. The latter can be facilitated by participation in a riot.

And we know that a violent act is not like the draining of an abscess but more like the activation of a granuloma. Results of Thematic Apperception Tests given to football players before and after a scrimmage show more hostile and violent imagery after the scrimmage than before.

A war as ambiguous in its goals and relentless in its pursuit as the one in Vietnam provides the opportunity for a massive provocation and rationalization of individual aggressive instincts. Once provoked, legitimized by National goals, sanctioned by Presidential authority, sustained by the omnipresence of brutal images and desensitized to human suffering, such aggressive instincts are capable of exploitation for any issue on any front. It is no accident of history that major riots occur during times of war.

We must be prepared to accept the possibility that whatever else is or is not done about our cities, the rioting will not end until the war does.

THE BAPTISM BY BEER

5

Permission to reprint the article originally titled "Tavern Culture: The Sustenance of Homeless Men," American Journal of Orthopsychiatry, Vol. XXXVII, No. 5, October, 1967, was furnished to the author by the American Journal of Orthopsychiatry.

1. Bogue, D. J., *Skid Row in American Cities*, Community and Family Study Center, University of Chicago, 1963. This is an extensive and classic study of homelessness focusing on Chicago's skid row. Along with illuminating data about the men and the institutions which exist symbiotically along the row are some fascinating vignettes and case histories. A major and possibly definitive contribution to the social science literature on homelessness is forthcoming from the Bureau of Applied Social Research of Columbia University. Professor Theodore Caplow and his co-workers have been exploring the field for over a decade under the sponsorship of the New York City Department of Welfare and the National Institute of Mental Health. See also Demone, Jr., H. W., and Blacker, E., *The Unattached and Socially Isolated Resident on Skid Row*, Boston Community Development Program, June, 1961. This unpublished report is an example of the type

of basic and modest survey that a city can undertake to begin an action program for such a population. D. Gottlieb's "The Neighborhood Tavern and the Cocktail Lounge, A Study of Class Differences" (*American Journal of Sociology*, Vol. LXII:559–562, 1957) is a very nice study documenting what should be intuitively known by anyone who occasionally wants to buy a drink at a "bar." There are different types of bars and they serve different functions. Finally, in *Skid Row as a Way of Life* (Totown, New Jersey, Bedminster Press, 1965) Dr. S. E. Wallace has written a beautiful and concise description of the scene on skid row as well as provided a model for participant observation as a sociological technique.

2. Chafetz, M. E., Blane, H. T., Abram, H. S., Golner, J., Lacy, E., McCourt, W. F., Clark, E., Meyers, W., "Establishing Treatment Relations with Alcoholics," *Journal of Nervous and Mental Disease*, Vol. CXXXIV: 395–409, 1962. This group of clinicians and researchers at the Massachusettes General Hospital has done much to dispel a sense of pessimism so widely shared by the mental health professions about the problem of alcoholism. An even more dramatic illustration of what can be done in the form of a research and intervention program for skid row men exists in Philadelphia. Under the direction of Irving Shandler, the Diagnostic and Relocation Center has demonstrated what sophistication, tireless dedication and imagination can do with an apparently hopeless clientele. The publications that will emerge from the activities of that center (largely supported by the Greater Philadelphia Movement and the National Institute of Mental Health) will have a major impact on all types of health and welfare programs, not just those directed to indigent alcoholics.

3. Gottlieb, *op. cit.*

5. Chafetz, M. E., *Liquor: The Servant of Man*, Boston, Little, Brown, 1965. Dr. Chafetz has found it necessary to state, through this delightful book, that one need not be an abstainer nor a moralist to be professionally concerned with problem drinking.

THE PSYCHIATRIST AS CREATIVE ARTIST

6

1. One of the great psychiatric papers of all time, one which provided a quantum jump to community psychiatry, was Dr. Erich Lindemann's report on his investigations of the grieving process in the aftermath of the Coconut Grove fire in Boston. This paper, "Symptomatology and Management of Acute Grief," can be found in *The American Journal of Psychiatry*, Vol. CI, pp. 141–148.

THE PSYCHIATRIST IN SPACE

7

1. Hediger, H., *Studies of the Psychology and Behavior of Captured Animals in Zoos and Circuses*, London, Butterworth and Co., 1955.

———, *Wild Animals in Captivity*, London, Butterworth and Co., 1950.

2. Christian, John J., "Factors in Mass Mortality of

a Herd of Sika Deer," *Chesapeake Science,* Vol. I, No. 2, June, 1960, pp. 79–95.

3. Calhoun, John B., "A Behavior Sink," in *Roots of Behavior,* edited by Eugene L. Bliss, New York, Harper and Row, 1962, Chapter 22.

———, "Population Density and Social Pathology," *Scientific American,* Vol. CCVI, February, 1962, pp. 139–146.

———, "The Study of Wild Animals under Controlled Conditions," *Annals of the New York Academy of Sciences,* Vol. LI, 1950.

4. Hauser, P. M., in an address to the 19th Annual Conference on Aging, University of Michigan, October, 1966.

5. Chombard de Lauwe, Paul, *Famille et Habitation,* Paris, Editions de Centre National de la Recherche Scientifique, 1959.

6. Hall, Edward T., *The Hidden Dimension,* Garden City, N.Y., Doubleday and Co., 1966.

———, *The Silent Language,* Garden City, N.Y., Doubleday and Co., 1959.

7. Osmond, Humphry, "The Relationship between Architect and Psychiatrist," in *Psychiatric Architecture,* edited by C. Goshen, Washington, D.C., American Psychiatric Association, 1959.

8. Sommer, Robert, "The Distance for Comfortable Conversations, a Further Study," *Sociometry,* Vol. XXV, 1962.

9. Dumont, M. P., et al, "Patient and Staff Reactions to a Change in Procedure on a Psychiatric Ward," *Diseases of the Nervous System,* Vol. IV, April, 1960.

10. Spivack, Mayer, "Sensory Distortions in Tunnels and Corridors," *Hospital and Community Psychiatry,*

American Psychiatric Association, January, 1967, pp. 24–30.

11. *Architecture for the Community Mental Health Center*, edited by Coryl L. Jones, Houston, Texas, Rice University and Mental Health Materials Center, Inc., 1967.

12. As an illustration of how one type of police training can obviate the need for guns, see *The Koga Method: Police Weaponless Control and Defense Techniques*, by Koga, R. K., and Nelson, J. G., Beverly Hills, Glencoe Press, 1967. Beware of the seductiveness of the "non-lethal" weapon idea for police officers. Apart from the fact that many of the gases being used are not innocuous, there is every indication that such weapons will not be used *instead* of guns but along with them and much *earlier* and more *vindictively* than guns would be utilized. Moreover, the availability of paralyzing gases, tranquilizer guns and other such instruments, at a time when the police are having trouble distinguishing between civil disobedience and civil disorder, raises some serious questions for a democratic society.

13. Goffman, Erving, *Asylums*, Chicago, Aldine, 1962.

THE MENTAL HEALTH OF ORGANIZATIONS

8

1. This paper appears in a concise and valuable publication entitled *Urban America and the Planning of Mental Health Services*, G.A.P. Symposium No. 10, New

York, Group for the Advancement of Psychiatry, 1964. For my review of this book see *Psychosomatic Medicine,* Vol. XXVII, No. 4, 1965.

2. A good overview and critique of this phenomenon can be found in a paper entitled "T-Group Education and Leadership Effectiveness: A Review of the Literature and a Critical Evaluation," by Robert J. House, available through the McKinsey Foundation for Management Research in New York.

3. A psychologist at Union College in Schenectady named Clare W. Graves has been adapting a theory of ethical values and a conceptual scheme of a hierarchy of human needs to business management. See his article "Deterioration of Work Standards," *Harvard Business Review,* September-October, 1966.

4. Michael Harrington, one of the men most responsible for turning America's face to the poor, wrote an article "The Social-Industrial Complex," for the November, 1967, issue of *Harper's Magazine.* Harrington finds something menacing in this new corporate conscience which acts as if satisfaction of social needs and making money go hand in hand. While it may not be menacing, the article by John T. Garrity in the May, 1968 issue of Harvard Business Review, entitled *Red Ink for Ghetto Industries?,* nicely demonstrates how a business mentality responds to a bill-of-fare of social justice. After costing out a program of job development for ghetto youths by a private industry, the author reminds business-men, as if he had to, that the creation of jobs for the ghetto "must be consistent with private enterprise's basic profit requirement."

5. For a distinction between the two schools of man-

agement, see "Human Relations or Human Resources," by Raymond Miles, in *Harvard Business Review*, July-August, 1965. The "X and Y" theories of management as discussed by Douglas McGregor in his book, *The Human Side of Enterprise*, New York, McGraw-Hill, 1960, distinguish between organizations based on authoritarian control and those based on a participating, egalitarian ideology. Also see the works of Warren Bennis for a description of nonbureaucratic organizations and also for the alleged role of T-groups in achieving organizational change.

6. Erik Erikson is now engaged in a study of Gandhi. As a promise of things to come, he presented, "Psychoanalysis and On-going History: Problems of Identity, Hatred and Nonviolence," *The American Journal of Psychiatry*, Vol. CXX, No. 3, September, 1965.

7. Before he became Secretary of the Department of Health, Education, and Welfare, where his ideas would be given the acid test, John W. Gardner wrote an article entitled, "How to Prevent Organizational Dry Rot," *Harper's Magazine*, October, 1965, in which he put forth nine rules for maintaining vitality in an organization. They dealt with recruitment of talent, a hospitable environment for the individual, provision for self-criticism, fluidity of internal structure, communication, nonregimentation, control of vestedness, future orientation, and motivation.

THE PHYSICIAN AND SOCIAL CHANGE

9

1. From *The Myth of Sisyphus*, New York, Vintage Books, 1955. How long will it be before all of us hear and understand his ideas?